GIFTS
THAT *taste* GOOD

Whatever the reason, whatever the season, receiving gifts is always a delight. And when the gifts are homemade and delivered in handcrafted packaging, they're extra special. Gifts That Taste Good is brimming with delicious recipes and thoughtful crafts that will bring that loving, handmade touch to all your gift-giving. It's a continuation of the wonderful ideas presented in Gifts of Good Taste, the first book in our Memories in the Making series.

*The titles for both volumes came from our belief that gifts of good taste **are** gifts that taste good. And your tremendous response to the first book let us know that you agree. May you receive much pleasure from this second collection. It's filled with wonderful ways to tell the special people in your life, "I know you well!"*

Anne Young

When I give I give myself.
— WALT WHITMAN

LEISURE ARTS
Little Rock, Arkansas

GIFTS THAT *taste* GOOD

EDITORIAL STAFF

Editor-in-Chief: Anne Van Wagner Young
Managing Editor: Sandra Graham Case
Creative Art Director: Gloria Bearden
Assistant Editor: Susan Frantz Wiles

PRODUCTION
Production Director: Sherry Taylor O'Connor
Food Editor: Christy Kalder
Production Assistant: Ginger A. Alumbaugh
Copy and Design Assistants: Kathy Rose Bradley, Patricia Wallenfang Sowers, and Diana Heien Suttle

EDITORIAL
Editorial Director: Dorothy Latimer Johnson
Editorial Assistant: Linda L. Trimble
Copy Assistants: Tammi Williamson Bradley, Marjorie Lacy Bishop, Eva Marie Delfos, Darla Burdette Kelsay, Sherry Lynn Lloyd, and Tena Kelley Vaughn

ART
Production Art Director: Melinda Stout
Production Artists: Linda Lovette, Cindy Zimmerebner-Nassab, Sondra Harrison Daniel, and Kathleen Murphy
Photo Stylist: Karen Smart Hall
Typesetters: Cindy Lumpkin and Stephanie Cordero

BUSINESS STAFF

Publisher: Steve Patterson
Controller: Tom Siebenmorgen
Retail Sales Director: Richard Tignor
Retail Marketing Director: Pam Stebbins
Retail Customer Services Director: Margaret Sweetin

Marketing Manager: Russ Barnett
Executive Director of Marketing and Circulation: Guy A. Crossley
Print Production: Nancy Reddick Lister and Laura Lockhart

MEMORIES IN THE MAKING SERIES

International Standard Book Number 0-942237-09-9

Table of Contents

CELEBRATING SPECIAL DAYS

I notice this, each year I live:
I always like the gifts I get,
But how I love the gifts I give!

— CAROLYN WELLS

*S*end best wishes for the new year with a jar of spicy Black-eyed Pea Dip. Flavored with sour cream and salsa, the dip is a tasty new way to observe the tradition of eating peas to ensure a year of prosperity. And it's sure to bring good luck in keeping those New Year's resolutions, too! For a fun presentation, decorate a market basket with goals for the year and include tortilla chips for dipping.

BLACK-EYED PEA DIP

 1 can (16 ounces) black-eyed peas, drained and divided
 3 green onions, chopped with tops included
 ½ cup sour cream
 1 teaspoon garlic salt
 ½ cup chunky-style salsa
 4 slices bacon, cooked and crumbled

Reserving ⅓ cup, place peas in a blender or food processor fitted with a steel blade. Process until smooth. Blend in onions, sour cream, and garlic salt. Transfer mixture to a bowl and stir in reserved peas and salsa. Garnish with bacon.

Yield: about 2 ½ cups of dip

RESOLUTION BASKET

You will need a market basket, black and white acrylic paint, matte clear acrylic spray, black and white paint markers, and foam brushes.

1. Use acrylic paint to paint body of basket white and handle and rim black; allow to dry.
2. Use white paint marker to write "I RESOLVE TO..." on handle and rim; allow to dry.
3. Use black paint marker to write resolutions on basket; allow to dry.
4. Spray basket with acrylic spray; allow to dry.

SUPER BOWL SNACKS

CHEDDAR BEER CHEESE

4 cups (16 ounces) grated sharp
   Cheddar cheese, room
   temperature
2 teaspoons Worcestershire sauce
1 clove garlic, minced
½ teaspoon hot pepper sauce
½ teaspoon dry mustard
½ teaspoon seasoned salt
¼ teaspoon ground black pepper
⅓ cup flat beer

Place all ingredients in a blender
or food processor fitted with a steel
blade. Process until smooth. Transfer
to serving container. Cover and
refrigerate overnight. Serve at room
temperature with crackers.

Yield: about 2 cups of spread

For pennant, we used a permanent
felt-tip marker to write ''SUPER
BOWL'' on a white felt triangle and
glued a blue felt band and streamers
to end of pennant. The pennant was
glued to a small wooden dowel.

*O*n Super Bowl Sunday,
*y*our favorite sports fan will give
a cheer for tangy Cheddar Beer
*C*heese. Teamed with crackers, it
*m*akes a hearty treat. For fun,
*t*uck the spread and some bottled
*d*rinks in a colorful ''super''
*b*owl. Fresh popcorn makes an
*u*nbeatable packing material
*t*hat's great for munching, too.
A mini pennant in team colors
*c*ompletes the gift.

MY CHOCOLATE VALENTINE

CHOCOHOLIC CAKE

Say "I love you" to someone dear on Valentine's Day with this luscious gift. The velvety cake is created by enhancing a packaged mix with pudding, sweet and semisweet chocolate, and sour cream. Crunchy pecans and chewy coconut hidden in the filling are a delicious surprise, and the dark fudge icing is sinfully rich. Topped with an elegant bouquet of sugared gumdrop roses and edged with paper lace, the cake sends a very special valentine message.

CAKE

- 1 box (18.25 ounces) butter fudge cake mix
- 1 package (4 ounces) instant chocolate pudding mix
- ½ cup vegetable oil
- ½ cup water
- 4 eggs
- 1 cup sour cream
- 1 bar (4 ounces) sweet chocolate, grated
- 1½ cups miniature semisweet chocolate chips

COCO-NUT CHOCOLATE FILLING

- 2 tablespoons cornstarch
- ½ cup granulated sugar
- ⅛ teaspoon salt
- ½ cup water
- 1 tablespoon butter or margarine
- 1 square (1 ounce) semisweet chocolate
- 1½ cups flaked coconut
- 1 cup chopped pecans

FUDGE ICING

- 2 cups granulated sugar
- ¼ cup plus 2 tablespoons cocoa
- ½ cup butter or margarine
- ½ cup milk
- 1 tablespoon light corn syrup
- 1 teaspoon vanilla extract
  Large red and green gumdrops for rose garnish

For cake, combine cake mix, pudding mix, oil, and water in a large bowl. Mix well. Add eggs one at a time, beating after each addition. Blend in sour cream. Stir in grated chocolate and chocolate chips.

Preheat oven to 350 degrees. Grease and flour two 8-inch square baking pans. Divide batter evenly into pans. Bake 40 to 50 minutes, checking for doneness with a toothpick. Remove from oven and cool 10 minutes in pans. (Cakes will be very moist.) Loosen edges of cakes with spatula and invert onto wire racks. Cool completely.

For filling, combine cornstarch, sugar, salt, and water in a small saucepan. Cook over medium heat, stirring constantly, until thickened and bubbly. Remove from heat and stir in butter and chocolate until melted. Cool slightly. Stir in coconut and pecans.

For icing, combine sugar and cocoa in a small saucepan, mixing well. Add butter, milk, and corn syrup. Bring to a boil and continue to boil 2 minutes, stirring constantly. Remove from heat and stir in vanilla; cool 5 minutes. Beat at medium speed with an electric mixer until thick enough to spread.

Spread filling on top of one layer of cake. Place second layer on top. Frost sides and top of cake with icing. Garnish with gumdrop roses.

To make each gumdrop rose, flatten 3 red gumdrops with a rolling pin on a lightly sugared surface into 1½-inch ovals. Dust flattened gumdrops with sugar and cut in half horizontally. Referring to photo, roll 1 half tightly to make center of rose. Wrap remaining halves around center, overlapping edges slightly. Gently squeeze rose together at the base to secure; trim base as needed. For each leaf, flatten 1 green gumdrop on a lightly sugared surface into a 1½-inch oval. Dust with sugar. Using a paring knife, cut leaf shape from flattened gumdrop.

Yield: one 2-layer cake

AN IRISH GIFT

*O*n St. Patrick's Day this year, give a taste of the Emerald Isle with Irish Coffee Balls. The delightful flavor of Irish coffee, captured in a chewy no-bake cookie, will add enjoyment to the day. For an elegant offering, present the cookies in an Irish coffee mug with a pretty napkin and a keepsake shamrock. And since it's more fun to celebrate with a friend, give a pair of mugs and cookies for two!

IRISH COFFEE BALLS

3½ cups vanilla wafer crumbs
1 cup finely chopped pecans
1½ cups sifted confectioners sugar, divided
3 tablespoons instant coffee granules
⅓ cup Irish whiskey
⅓ cup light corn syrup

In a large bowl, combine cookie crumbs, pecans, and 1 cup sugar. In a small cup, dissolve coffee granules in Irish whiskey. Add to dry mixture along with corn syrup, mixing until well blended. Shape mixture into 1-inch balls. Roll in remaining sugar. Store in airtight container.

Yield: about 4½ dozen cookies

Note: Cookies become more flavorful after sitting 2 to 3 days.

For shamrock, hot glue eucalyptus leaves to a small twig and spray lightly with gold spray paint.

April Fool!

A friend who's "full of baloney" will get a kick out of this April Fools' Day gift! Humorously presented in a small plastic garbage can, our Pickled Bologna is great for snacking — and its tangy flavor will appeal to grown-ups and kids alike. A bright tag cut in an "explosive" shape makes a fun finish.

PICKLED BOLOGNA

     2 rolls (14 ounces each)
           beef bologna
     4 cups vinegar
     1 onion, sliced
     1 lemon, sliced
     2 tablespoons pickling spice
     1 bay leaf
     2 cloves garlic, minced
     ½ teaspoon whole black
           peppercorns
     ¼ teaspoon crushed red pepper
           flakes

Cut bologna into 1-inch thick slices; quarter each slice. Place in a sterilized ½-quart jar.

In a medium saucepan, combine remaining ingredients. Bring to a boil and simmer 8 minutes. Remove from heat and pour over bologna to within 1 inch of top of the jar. Seal jar and let stand at room temperature 1 week before serving. Store in refrigerator after opening.

Yield: about 1 ½ quarts of bologna

BUNNY BASKET

*W*ith her lap overflowing with delicious candy eggs, our sweet-faced bunny miss will delight someone special on Easter morning. The White Chocolate Cream Eggs, filled with rich vanilla-pecan nougat, are gently speckled with food coloring to create a pastel look. The bunny basket will continue to provide a breath of spring long after the candy is eaten.

WHITE CHOCOLATE CREAM EGGS

½ cup butter or margarine
2 cups finely chopped pecans
3 cups sifted confectioners sugar
⅔ cup sweetened condensed milk
1 teaspoon vanilla extract
8 ounces white chocolate, broken
  into small pieces
  Paste food coloring

In a large saucepan, melt butter. Stir in pecans, sugar, milk, and vanilla, blending well. Transfer to a bowl, cover, and chill 2 to 3 hours.

Shape candy mixture into 1½-inch long egg shapes and place on waxed paper-lined baking sheets. Cover and refrigerate overnight.

To dip chocolate successfully, follow Kitchen Tips, page 120, to melt and temper chocolate. Use a fondue fork to dip candy eggs into melted chocolate. Place on wire racks with waxed paper underneath. Allow coating to harden.

To speckle eggs, place a small amount of food coloring on a paper plate. Crumple a small square of waxed paper and dip into food coloring; blot on plate. Gently stamp candy egg to make speckles. Using a paper towel, carefully blot egg to absorb heavy spots of food coloring. Repeat with remaining colors. Let eggs sit uncovered in a cool place (do not refrigerate) until dry.

Yield: about 2½ dozen candy eggs

BUNNY BASKET

You will need one approx. 8″ dia. basket; ½ yd of 38″w unbleached muslin for bunny; ½ yd of 44″w fabric for clothing; ¼″w elastic; 1¾ yds of 1¼″w pre-gathered eyelet trim; pink, blue, and grey embroidery floss; tracing paper; hot glue gun; glue sticks; thread to match fabrics; ecru quilting thread; five 12″ lengths of ⅜″w ribbon; polyester fiberfill; seam ripper; and fabric marking pencil.

1. Use body, ear, and foot patterns and follow Transferring Patterns, page 122. For each shape, cut two pieces of muslin 1″ larger on all sides than pattern. Follow Sewing Shapes, page 122, to make one body, two ears, and two feet from muslin. Stuff body and feet with fiberfill. Sew final closures of all shapes by hand.

2. (Note: Use 6 strands of floss throughout.) Use blue floss to work French Knots for eyes, pink floss to work French Knot for nose, and grey floss to work Straight Stitch for mouth.

3. For whiskers, thread needle with three 7″ lengths of quilting thread. Run needle through face; unthread needle. Knot lengths together on each side of face.

4. For toes, thread needle with pink floss; knot one end. Bring needle through foot at one ●, over top of foot, and back through foot, coming out at same ●; pull floss tight. Repeat to make a second stitch at same ●; knot and secure floss ends. Repeat for remaining ●'s.

5. For each ear, baste along short edge and pull basting threads to gather ear to 1″. Whipstitch ears to body at seamline. Remove basting threads.

6. For height of skirt piece, measure height of basket and add ¾″. For width of skirt piece, measure circumference of basket and double the measurement. Cut fabric the determined height and width, piecing if necessary.

7. Cut a piece of eyelet trim the same length as one long edge of skirt piece. Matching right sides and straight edges, use a ¼″ seam allowance to sew eyelet to one long edge of skirt. Press seam allowance toward skirt. Topstitch on skirt fabric close to seam.

8. Matching right sides and short edges, fold skirt piece in half. Using a ¼″ seam allowance, sew short edges together.

9. For casing, press remaining raw edge of skirt piece under ½″; stitch ⅜″ from pressed edge. On wrong side of skirt, cut a small slit through one layer of casing. Cut elastic the circumference of the basket plus 1″. Thread elastic through casing and overlap ends; stitch in place.

10. For blouse, cut one 9″ x 20″ piece of fabric. Press each short edge of fabric under ¼″; press under ¼″ again and stitch in place. Matching right sides, fold fabric in half lengthwise and sew long edges together. Press seam open. For neck opening, use seam ripper to rip a 5″ opening along center of seam. Baste around opening ¼″ from edge. Turn right side out.

11. Place blouse on body; pull basting threads, gathering fabric around neck. Knot thread and trim ends. Cut eyelet trim to fit around neck. Glue eyelet and one ribbon around neck. Tie one ribbon into a bow and glue at neck. Tie one ribbon into a bow around each sleeve.

12. Glue feet and skirt to basket. Glue body to top edge of basket.

13. Tie ribbon around one ear.

FOR MOTHER

A box of creamy White Chocolate Truffles is a sweet way to say "I love you" on Mother's Day. And while Mom is savoring the rich confections, she's sure to admire your handcrafted keepsake box decorated with wrapping paper.

WHITE CHOCOLATE TRUFFLES

 8 ounces white chocolate, broken into small pieces
¼ cup butter
½ cup sifted confectioners sugar
 1 egg yolk
 2 tablespoons créme de cacao liqueur, optional
 1 cup chopped blanched almonds, lightly toasted

Melt chocolate and butter in the top of a double boiler over low heat, stirring constantly. Remove from heat. Add sugar, egg yolk, and liqueur; beat with an electric mixer until smooth. Transfer mixture to a shallow glass casserole dish. Cover and refrigerate 1 hour.

Shape mixture into 1-inch balls; roll in almonds. Cover and refrigerate at least 8 hours. Serve truffles in miniature foil cups at room temperature. Store in airtight container in refrigerator.

Yield: about 2 dozen truffles

MOTHER'S DAY BOX

You will need an oval Shaker box; colored paper to cover box lid; gift wrap; tracing paper; graphite transfer paper; felt-tip calligraphy pen with medium point; matte clear acrylic spray; foam brushes; small, sharp scissors; satin ribbon to fit around rim of box lid; fabric glue; and matte Mod Podge® sealer.

1. Using box lid as a pattern, draw an oval on colored paper; do not cut out.
2. Trace "Mother" pattern onto tracing paper. Use transfer paper to transfer "Mother" to center of oval. Use pen to write over "Mother."
3. (Note: Allow acrylic spray or Mod Podge® to dry between coats throughout.) Spray oval with three coats of acrylic spray. Cut out oval. Use Mod Podge® to glue oval to top of lid. Apply one coat of Mod Podge® to top of lid.
4. Cut motifs from gift wrap. Use Mod Podge® to glue motifs to top of lid. Apply three more coats of Mod Podge® to top of lid.
5. Use fabric glue to glue ribbon around rim of lid.
6. For side of box, measure circumference of box and add 1"; measure height of box. Cut gift wrap the determined measurements. Use Mod Podge® to glue gift wrap around box, overlapping ends.
7. Apply three coats of Mod Podge® to box.

FOR DAD

*O*n his special day, surprise
Dad with a treasure box filled
with distinctive Smoky Cheese
Bites. Smoked Cheddar cheese and
hickory-smoked almonds give the
snacks a rich, savory flavor.
To make the box, we simply glued
wrapping paper to a wooden
Shaker box and arranged cutout
motifs around the name on the
lid. The wide variety of paper
available today makes it easy to
find one just right for your Dad.
He's sure to appreciate such a
personalized gift!

SMOKY CHEESE BITES

    2 cups all-purpose flour
    ½ teaspoon salt
    ¼ teaspoon cayenne pepper
    2 cups (8 ounces) grated smoked
       Cheddar cheese
    1 cup butter or margarine, softened
    1 can (6 ounces) hickory-flavored
       whole almonds

In a large bowl, combine flour, salt,
and pepper. Add cheese, mixing well.
Cut in butter until mixture resembles a
coarse meal. Knead dough with hands
until smooth.

Preheat oven to 425 degrees. On a
lightly floured surface, roll out dough
to ¼-inch thickness. Cut into rounds
with a 1½-inch biscuit cutter.

Transfer rounds to greased baking
sheets, topping each with an almond.
Bake 10 to 12 minutes or until lightly
browned around edges. Cool on wire
racks. Store in airtight container.

Yield: about 5 dozen cheese bites

FATHER'S DAY BOX

For box, use "DAD" pattern and
follow Mother's Day Box instructions,
page 16.

SUMMER'S BOUNTY

These Miniature Fruit Tarts are a luscious way to celebrate the bounty of summer! Topped with colorful fruit and berries, a rich vanilla cream filling is nestled in flaky pastry shells. For a sweet summer gift, arrange a selection of tarts on an airy wicker plate and present them to a friend.

MINIATURE FRUIT TARTS

PASTRY
- ½ cup confectioners sugar
- ¼ teaspoon salt
- ½ cup butter, cut into pieces and softened
- 2 egg yolks, beaten
- 3 tablespoons cold water
- 2 cups all-purpose flour

FILLING
- ¾ cup vanilla milk chips
- 3 tablespoons whipping cream
- 4 ounces cream cheese, softened
  Assorted fresh fruits: bananas, blueberries, grapes, kiwis, mandarin oranges, or strawberries.

GLAZE
- ⅔ cup apple jelly
- 2 teaspoons granulated sugar

For pastry, combine sugar and salt in a bowl. Cut in butter with a pastry blender or 2 knives until almost blended. Combine egg yolks and water in a small bowl; stir into butter mixture. Add flour, mixing just until blended. Divide dough in half and wrap in plastic wrap. Refrigerate at least 1 hour.

Preheat oven to 350 degrees. Working with half of the dough at a time, press about 1 tablespoon of dough into each small tart pan. Prick bottoms and sides of shells with a fork. Place on baking sheets and bake 20 to 25 minutes or until lightly browned. Cool on wire rack.

For filling, melt vanilla chips with cream in a double boiler over medium heat, stirring until smooth. Remove from heat and beat in cream cheese. Spoon filling into cooled pastry shells.

Referring to photo, decorate with assorted fruits. For glaze, melt jelly and sugar in a small saucepan over low heat; cool slightly. Brush gently over fruits. Chill several hours before serving.

Yield: about 18 tarts

WATERMELON DAYS

*W*ith our spicy Pickled Watermelon Rind, you can preserve some of the fun of a summertime watermelon festival. Perfect for snacks or with meals, the sweet, tangy morsels are real crowd-pleasers — and our recipe makes plenty for sharing. Pack this old-fashioned treat in canning jars topped with pink fabric "fruit" and black button "seeds" to deliver to friends and neighbors. Paper melon slices make cute gift tags.

PICKLED WATERMELON RIND

1   medium watermelon, about 16 pounds
2   tablespoons salt
3   (3 or 4-inch) cinnamon sticks, broken into pieces
1   tablespoon whole allspice
1   tablespoon whole cloves
4   cups vinegar
8   cups granulated sugar
1   lemon, thinly sliced

Remove rind from watermelon. Cut rind into 2-inch squares and remove peel with a paring knife. Place peeled rind in a Dutch oven and cover with water. Add salt and simmer over medium heat until rind is tender, about 25 to 30 minutes; drain. Transfer rind to a large bowl and cover with cold water. Cover bowl and refrigerate at least 4 hours; drain.

Wrap spices in a small square of cheesecloth; tie with kitchen twine. In a Dutch oven, bring vinegar and sugar to a boil. Add rind, spice bag, and lemon. Simmer until rind is transparent, about 35 to 45 minutes. Remove rind with a slotted spoon and pack into hot, sterilized pint jars. Bring syrup to a boil, remove spice bag, and pour hot syrup over rind through a sieve. Seal jars immediately.

Yield: about 5 to 6 pints of rind

WATERMELON TAGS AND JARS

For each tag, use colored pencils to decorate a half-circle of paper and write the name with a felt-tip pen. Tie tag to completed jar with $\frac{1}{16}''$ wide ribbon.

For each jar, you will need a canning jar and lid with screw ring, one 5" square of pink fabric, one 5" square of craft batting, eight ¼" dia. black buttons, flat paintbrush, lt green and dk green acrylic paint, matte clear acrylic spray, and craft glue.

1. Paint side of screw ring dk green and top of screw ring lt green; allow to dry. Spray ring with acrylic spray; allow to dry.
2. Using flat piece of lid as a pattern, cut a circle from fabric and batting. Glue batting to top of flat piece. Glue fabric to batting along fabric edge. Glue lid inside screw ring.
3. Glue buttons to top of lid; allow to dry.

Hurray For The Red, White, And Blue!

*T*op off a Fourth of July cookout with these red, white, and blue dessert sauces! Perfect for serving over ice cream or pound cake, the toppings are flavored with tart cherries, creamy white chocolate, and spirited blueberries. For sharing, cap the jars with our patriotic lids and take along a freezer of homemade ice cream.

BLUEBERRY SAUCE

⅓ cup granulated sugar
½ teaspoon ground cinnamon
2 tablespoons cornstarch
1 tablespoon lemon juice
1 package (16 ounces) frozen
     blueberries, thawed and
     drained with juice reserved
3 tablespoons bourbon, optional

In a saucepan, combine sugar, cinnamon, and cornstarch. Stir in lemon juice and ½ cup reserved juice, blending well. Bring to a boil; reduce heat to low and simmer 5 minutes, stirring frequently. Remove from heat and stir in blueberries and bourbon. Serve warm over ice cream or pound cake. Store in airtight container in refrigerator.

Yield: about 2 cups of sauce

CHERRY SAUCE

- 1 can (16 ounces) pitted tart
     cherries, drained with juice
     reserved
- ⅓ cup granulated sugar
- 1 tablespoon cornstarch
- 2 tablespoons grenadine
- ¼ teaspoon almond extract

Coarsely chop cherries; set aside. In a saucepan, combine sugar and cornstarch. Stir in ¼ cup reserved juice and grenadine, blending well. Bring to a boil; reduce heat to low and simmer 5 minutes, stirring frequently. Remove from heat; stir in cherries and almond extract. Serve warm over ice cream or pound cake. Store in airtight container in refrigerator.

Yield: about 1½ cups of sauce

WHITE CHOCOLATE SAUCE

- 1 cup whipping cream
- 10 ounces white chocolate, coarsely
     chopped and divided
- 2 tablespoons light corn syrup
- ⅓ cup half and half

In a small saucepan, heat cream over medium heat just to boiling. Remove from heat. Reserving ⅓ cup chocolate, add remaining chocolate and corn syrup to cream. With a wire whisk, blend until smooth. Pour into a small bowl; stir in half and half. Cover and refrigerate at least 3 hours. Stir in remaining chocolate. Serve chilled over ice cream. Store in airtight container in refrigerator.

Yield: about 2 cups of sauce

PATRIOTIC JARS

You will need three half-pint canning jars and lids with screw rings; scraps of red, ecru, and blue fabrics; ivory, blue, and red spray paint; Design Master® glossy wood tone spray; craft glue; two 1″w wooden stars; small ivory buttons; 23″ of ecru cotton yarn; red, white, and blue embroidery floss (use 2 strands throughout); craft batting; removable fabric marking pen; black permanent felt-tip pen with fine point; and tracing paper.

STAR JAR LID
1. Spray screw ring with red paint, then wood tone spray, allowing to dry between coats.
2. Use flat piece of lid as a pattern and cut one circle from ecru fabric and batting.
3. Use fabric marking pen to draw a 1¾″ wide star on right side of fabric circle. Use red floss and Running Stitch, page 124, to stitch star. Use blue floss to sew a button in center of star. Remove pen lines. Glue batting to flat piece of lid. Glue fabric circle to batting along fabric edge. Glue lid inside ring.
4. Tear a ½″ x 20″ strip from blue fabric. Tie strip into a bow around lid.

FLAG JAR LID
1. Spray screw ring with blue paint, then wood tone spray, allowing to dry between coats.
2. Cut a 4″ square from a striped piece of fabric and a 1¾″ square from blue fabric. Fringe edges of blue square approximately ⅛″. Matching edges, place blue square on upper left corner of striped fabric to resemble a flag. Use white floss and Running Stitch, page 124, to stitch squares together along edges of blue square.
3. Using flat piece of lid as a pattern, cut one circle from "flag" and batting. Glue batting to flat piece of lid. Glue fabric circle to batting along fabric edge. Glue lid inside ring.
4. Spray stars with ivory paint, then wood tone spray, allowing to dry between coats. Glue a button to front of each star. Cut a 21″ length of yarn; glue one star to each end of yarn. Tie yarn into a bow around lid.

HEART JAR LID
1. Spray screw ring with ivory paint, then wood tone spray, allowing to dry between coats.
2. Use flat piece of lid as a pattern and cut one circle from blue fabric and batting. Glue batting to flat piece of lid. Glue fabric circle to batting along fabric edge. Glue lid inside ring.
3. Trace large and small heart patterns onto tracing paper and cut out. Use patterns and cut one large heart from red fabric and one small heart from ecru fabric. Use black pen to write "My Country 'tis of thee" on small heart. Glue large heart, then small heart, to lid; glue two buttons to lid.
4. For firecracker, cut a 1¼″ x 3½″ piece of red fabric and a 2″ piece of yarn. Beginning at one short edge of fabric, tightly wrap fabric around one end of yarn; glue to secure. Glue firecracker to lid.
5. For trim on screw ring, cut a ⅞″ x 9½″ piece of red fabric. Press long edges ¼″ to wrong side; glue strip around lid.

FRIENDSHIP DAY

*On Friendship Day
(the first Sunday in August),
send fudgy greetings to a
beloved friend. Our Mint
Brownie Bites are bursting
with chunks of chocolate
mint candy and walnuts.
A chocolate-brown basket
with a minty green wash
and a no-sew liner are
perfect for delivering your
sweet wishes.*

MINT BROWNIE BITES

4 ounces unsweetened chocolate
1 cup butter or margarine
3 eggs
1 cup granulated sugar
1 cup brown sugar, firmly packed
1 teaspoon vanilla extract
¼ teaspoon almond extract
1 cup all-purpose flour
¼ teaspoon salt
¾ cup chopped walnuts
⅔ cup chopped Andes® chocolate
    mint wafer candies
    Mint-flavored candy melts for
        decoration, optional

In a small saucepan, melt chocolate
and butter over low heat, stirring
until smooth. Remove from heat and
cool completely.

Preheat oven to 350 degrees. In
a large bowl, beat eggs and sugars
3 minutes or until thick and creamy.
Stir in extracts and chocolate mixture.
Add flour and salt, stirring until
mixture is completely blended. Stir in
walnuts and chopped candies. Spoon
batter into buttered miniature muffin
pans, filling pans two-thirds full. Bake
15 to 20 minutes or until brownies
begin to pull away from sides of pans.
Cool completely before removing
from pans.

To decorate with melted candy,
follow Kitchen Tips, page 120.
Referring to photo, drizzle melted
candy over tops of brownies. Store in
airtight container.

Yield: about 4 dozen brownies

MINTY BASKET AND NO-SEW FABRIC LINER

You will need a dark brown basket
(we used a 6½″ x 8½″ basket),
mint green acrylic paint, foam brush,
a soft cloth, matte clear acrylic spray,
one 18″ square of fabric, four 18″
lengths of ⅛″w satin ribbon, and
Slomon's Stitchless Fabric Glue.

1. Spray basket with acrylic spray;
allow to dry. Mix 2 parts paint to
1 part water. Paint basket with diluted
paint and remove excess with soft
cloth; allow to dry. Spray basket with
acrylic spray; allow to dry.
2. For liner, glue ribbon lengths to
fabric 1½″ from each edge; allow to
dry. Press edges of fabric ½″ to
wrong side; press ½″ to wrong side
again and glue in place. Allow to dry.

A "Picnic Kind Of Day"

Help a special family enjoy a "picnic kind of day" with these tangy marinated carrots. Chilled and served as a salad, our Picnic Carrots have a light, refreshing flavor. To present your dish, stencil a bevy of carrot-lovin' bunnies on a little basket and gift tag. Tuck in a jar of the carrots and add a border of gingham ribbon for a country finish.

PICNIC CARROTS

- 2 pounds carrots
- 3 green onions, sliced with tops included
- ½ cup chopped green pepper
- 1 can (10¾ ounces) tomato soup, undiluted
- ¾ cup granulated sugar
- ½ cup vegetable oil
- ½ cup vinegar
- 1 tablespoon Worcestershire sauce
- 1 teaspoon salt
- ⅛ teaspoon cayenne pepper

Wash, peel, and slice carrots. Steam until crisp-tender. Drain. Place in a bowl with onions and green pepper.

In a medium saucepan, combine remaining ingredients. Bring to a boil, stirring constantly. Pour over carrot mixture. Cover and refrigerate at least 24 hours before serving.

Yield: about 6 cups of carrots

STENCILED BASKET AND TAG

You will need a basket with area suitable for stenciling (we used a 1 qt. berry basket), brown acrylic paint, craft glue, ribbon to fit around rim of basket, tagboard (manila folder), tracing paper, craft knife, small stencil brush, paper towels, green felt-tip pen with fine point, graphite transfer paper, and matte clear acrylic spray.

1. Spray basket with three coats of acrylic spray, allowing to dry between coats.
2. For tag, cut a 3" x 1½" piece of tagboard.

3. For bunnies on basket and tag, follow How To Stencil, page 122.
4. Use pen to write "HAVE A PICNIC!" on tag and to draw grass on basket.
5. Spray basket with acrylic spray; allow to dry.
6. Glue ribbon around rim of basket.

AUTUMN'S BOUNTY

*C*elebrate the bounty of autumn with a loaf of sweet Orange Yeast Bread served with creamy Honey-Orange Butter! The spicy golden bread is filled with orange slice candies, nuts, and raisins. For a special presentation, cradle the bread in our quilted bread cloth and include a muslin-topped jar of the butter. We took our cue from the fall leaves to create the simple quilting pattern. A rustic basket makes an attractive carrier.

ORANGE YEAST BREAD

BREAD

½ cup golden raisins
3 tablespoons orange-flavored liqueur
¼ cup butter or margarine
½ cup milk
¼ cup granulated sugar
½ teaspoon salt
1 envelope active dry yeast
½ teaspoon granulated sugar
¼ cup warm water
1 egg
1 egg yolk
3 to 4 cups all-purpose flour
1 teaspoon ground cinnamon
½ teaspoon ground nutmeg
¼ teaspoon ground cloves
¼ teaspoon ground allspice
⅓ cup diced orange slice candies
⅓ cup chopped almonds, toasted
⅓ cup pine nuts
1 tablespoon grated orange peel

GLAZE

¼ cup light corn syrup
¼ cup fresh orange juice
1 tablespoon water
¼ teaspoon ground cinnamon
1 tablespoon butter or margarine

For bread, soak raisins in liqueur 30 minutes. In a small saucepan, melt butter with milk over low heat. Add ¼ cup sugar and salt. Cool slightly.

In a large bowl, combine yeast, ½ teaspoon sugar, and warm water. Cover with a towel and let stand 5 minutes. Add milk mixture to yeast. Beat in egg and egg yolk. In a separate bowl, sift together 3 cups flour and spices. Stir 2 cups flour mixture into yeast mixture, blending until smooth. Toss 1 tablespoon flour mixture with candies, nuts, and orange peel. Stir into dough with raisins and liqueur. Blend in remaining flour mixture until a soft dough forms.

Turn out dough onto a floured surface and knead until smooth, about 5 minutes. Knead in remaining flour as needed. Place dough in a large, buttered bowl, turning dough to coat all sides. Cover with plastic wrap and a towel. Let rise in a warm place until doubled in bulk, about 2 hours.

For glaze, combine corn syrup, orange juice, water, and cinnamon in a small saucepan. Cook over medium heat 5 minutes. Stir in butter and set aside to cool.

Punch down dough; knead again 5 minutes. Cover and let rest 10 minutes. Line a baking sheet with a brown paper bag. Shape dough into a 2-inch thick round. Place on baking sheet. Brush loaf with glaze. Cover and let rise 45 minutes.

Preheat oven to 350 degrees. Brush loaf again with glaze. Bake 40 to 50 minutes until loaf is golden brown and sounds hollow when tapped. Cool completely on a wire rack before slicing. Serve toasted with Honey-Orange Butter.

Yield: one 9-inch round loaf

HONEY-ORANGE BUTTER

½ cup butter or margarine, softened
¼ cup honey
2 tablespoons fresh orange juice
1 tablespoon grated orange peel

In a small bowl, blend all ingredients until smooth. Cover and refrigerate at least 2 hours. Bring to room temperature before serving.

Yield: about 1 cup of spread

QUILTED BREAD CLOTH

You will need two 18½″ squares of unbleached muslin, one 18½″ square of polyester bonded batting, tracing paper, dressmaker's carbon, removable fabric marking pen, ecru quilting thread, ecru sewing thread, and 2⅛ yds of ecru extra-wide double-fold bias tape.

1. Trace pattern onto tracing paper. With edges of pattern 1″ from edges of one muslin square, use dressmaker's carbon to transfer pattern to one corner of square. Use fabric marking pen to mark a 6″ square in center of muslin square.
2. Place batting on remaining muslin square. Place marked muslin square, marked side up, on batting. Baste layers together from corner to corner and from side to side. Use quilting thread and a small Running Stitch, page 124, to quilt along marked lines. Remove carbon and pen lines.
3. Following manufacturer's instructions, apply bias tape to edges of bread cloth. Remove basting threads and press.

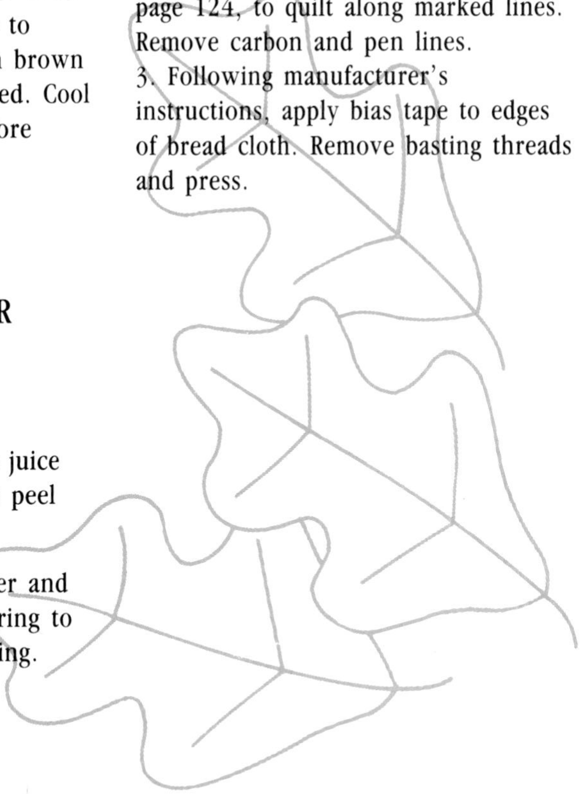

A NEIGHBORLY GIFT

*O*n *National Good Neighbor Day (the fourth Sunday in September), show a little kindness to someone nearby with a jar of rich, creamy Pecan Butter Spread. Delicious served with fruit or sweet crackers topped with Roasted Pecans, the spread is a luscious blend of Brie, cream cheese, sherry, and pecans. To dress up your gift, cover the jar lid and a Chinese food take-out carton with matching wrapping paper. Tuck the jar in the box with the pecans as packing material, and your gift will spread lots of goodwill!*

PECAN BUTTER SPREAD

1 ¼ cups chopped pecans
2 tablespoons peanut oil
8 ounces Brie cheese
1 package (3 ounces) cream cheese, softened
2 tablespoons sherry
¼ teaspoon salt

Place pecans and peanut oil in a blender or food processor fitted with a steel blade. Process to a smooth paste. Remove rind from Brie and add to pecan mixture with remaining ingredients. Process until mixture is completely blended. Store in airtight container in refrigerator. Serve at room temperature with wheatmeal biscuits or sliced apples. Top with Roasted Pecans.

Yield: about 1 ½ cups of spread

ROASTED PECANS

1 cup pecan halves
1 tablespoon butter or margarine, melted
   Salt

Preheat oven to 200 degrees. In a small bowl, combine pecans and butter. Pour nuts onto a baking sheet and bake 1 hour, stirring every 15 minutes. Drain on a paper towel-lined plate and sprinkle with salt. Cool completely. Store in airtight container.

Yield: 1 cup of pecans

For container, use a Chinese food take-out carton and follow Gift Box 2 instructions, page 123. We used a 2 ¾ " x 3 ¾ " x 4 ¼ " carton and decorated it with ½ "w ribbon.

BY THE LIGHT OF THE MOON

When the harvest moon sheds its light on cool autumn nights, a special friend can enjoy the long evenings while lingering over a cup of cappuccino. Our instant mix, flavored with chocolate, cinnamon, and nutmeg, makes it easy to enjoy the rich flavor of this Italian beverage. To deliver the late-night gift, adorn a rustic bag and basket with moon and star ornaments made of dried orange peel.

INSTANT CAPPUCCINO MIX

   1 cup powdered chocolate
      milk mix
   ¾ cup powdered non-dairy creamer
   ½ cup instant coffee granules
   ½ teaspoon ground cinnamon
   ¼ teaspoon ground nutmeg

  In a medium bowl, combine all ingredients. Store in airtight container.

Yield: about 2¼ cups of mix

To serve: Place 1 heaping tablespoon mix in a cup or mug. Add 1 cup boiling water and stir.

ORANGE PEEL PROJECTS

You will need a basket with handles, one 16½″ x 10½″ piece of fabric for bag, thread to match fabric, fresh orange peels, paring knife, tracing paper, waxed paper, large needle, books (to weight shapes while drying), and cotton yarn.

1. Trace patterns onto tracing paper and cut out. For each orange shape, flatten orange peel and use knife to cut around pattern.
2. Place shapes between two layers of waxed paper. Weight shapes with books for two days. Remove shapes and allow to air dry. If shapes begin to curl, weight with books again. If necessary, repeat until shapes are thoroughly dried.
3. Use yarn and Running Stitch, page 124, to string shapes together; tie ends of yarn to handles of basket.
4. For bag, use fabric and follow Step 2 of Fabric Bag instructions, page 122; turn bag right side out. Beginning in center on one side of bag (front), use yarn and a long Running Stitch to stitch 2″ from top of bag. Fringe top of bag ½″. Place a plastic bag of cappuccino mix in fabric bag and tie yarn into a bow. Thread each end of yarn through top of an orange shape and knot end; trim ends if necessary.

CREEPY COOKIES

Children will love helping brew up a batch of creepy cookies for their friends at Halloween. Our bats, jack-o'-lanterns, ghosts, and spiders are frightfully easy to create. Simply dress up purchased cookies with confectionery coatings and then let the kids assemble and decorate them with candy. To present the spooky creatures, turn disposable cups into "boo buckets" and line them with colorful napkins.

CHOCOLATE SPIDERS

 1 package (12 ounces)
   Twizzlers® chocolate-flavored
   twist candy
 4 ounces milk chocolate-flavored
   candy melts

Cut twist candy into 1½-inch pieces; slice each piece in half lengthwise. For each spider, refer to photo and place 8 candy pieces in a circle on a piece of waxed paper. Repeat with remaining candy pieces.

Melt candy melts following package instructions. Drop about 1 teaspoon of melted candy at center of each spider, connecting candy pieces. Use a toothpick to smooth melted candy into a uniform circle. Cool completely before removing from waxed paper.

Yield: about 2 dozen candies

FUDGY BAT COOKIES

 1 package (9 ounces) chocolate
   wafer cookies
 4 ounces milk chocolate-flavored
   candy melts

Use a serrated knife to carefully cut 18 of the cookies into quarters. Save remaining cookies for another use. For each bat, refer to photo and place 2 cookie quarters ¼-inch apart on waxed paper. Repeat with remaining quarters.

Melt candy melts following package instructions. Drop about ½ teaspoon of melted candy at center of each bat, connecting cookies. Use a toothpick to smooth melted candy into a uniform circle. Cool completely before removing from waxed paper.

Yield: about 3 dozen cookies

GHOST COOKIES

 6 ounces vanilla-flavored
   almond bark
 1 package (15.5 ounces)
   peanut-shaped peanut butter
   sandwich cookies
   Small black jelly beans

Melt almond bark following package instructions. Dip two-thirds of each cookie in melted candy, shaking gently to remove excess coating. Place on wire rack with waxed paper underneath. For eyes, cut jelly beans in half and refer to photo to place on cookies. Cool completely before removing from rack.

Yield: about 32 cookies

JACK-O'-LANTERN COOKIES

 1 package (9 ounces) chocolate
   wafer cookies
 ½ cup smooth peanut butter
 24 ounces vanilla-flavored
   almond bark
   Orange paste food coloring
   Black licorice candy

Spread a small amount of peanut butter on the bottom (flat side) of half of the cookies; top with remaining cookies. For faces, refer to photo and cut licorice into small triangles and squares.

Melt almond bark following package instructions. Remove from heat and tint with food coloring. Using tongs, dip each sandwich cookie in melted candy, coating completely. Gently shake each cookie to remove excess coating. Place on wire rack with waxed paper underneath. Place licorice pieces on the cookies for faces. Cool completely before removing from rack.

Yield: about 20 cookies

BOO BUCKETS

You will need plastic foam cups, orange and black spray paint, black and white acrylic paint, ⅛"w orange and black ribbon, small paintbrush, large needle, and paper napkins.

1. Spray paint outside of each cup; allow to dry.
2. Use acrylic paint to paint "BOO!" on each cup; allow to dry.
3. For each cup handle, use needle to thread ribbon ends through each side of cup; knot ribbon ends on inside of cup.
4. Place a napkin in each cup.

THANKSGIVING BASKET

These Sweet Potato Corn Sticks are perfect to take along when you're invited to someone's home for Thanksgiving dinner. A unique combination of sweet potatoes and cornbread, the lightly sweetened, cinnamon-spiced sticks are delicious served warm with butter. For a thoughtful hostess gift, present them in a pretty basket lined with a redwork cloth.

SWEET POTATO CORN STICKS

1 ½ cups cooked, peeled, and mashed sweet potatoes (about 2 medium potatoes)
½ cup buttermilk
⅓ cup butter or margarine, melted
2 eggs
1 cup yellow cornmeal
1 cup all-purpose flour
⅓ cup granulated sugar
2 ½ teaspoons baking powder
1 teaspoon ground cinnamon
½ teaspoon ground allspice
½ teaspoon salt

Preheat oven to 400 degrees. Brush cast-iron corn stick pan generously with vegetable oil; heat in oven 10 minutes.

In a large bowl, combine sweet potatoes, buttermilk, butter, and eggs, mixing until smooth. In a separate bowl, combine remaining ingredients. Add to sweet potato mixture, stirring just until combined. Fill prepared pan two-thirds full with batter. Bake 15 to 20 minutes or until browned around the edges. Serve warm with butter.

Yield: about 2 ½ dozen corn sticks

Note: To reheat corn sticks, wrap in aluminum foil and bake 10 minutes at 400 degrees.

REDWORK BREAD CLOTH

You will need red embroidery floss, two 15 ½ " squares of white medium weight 50 % linen/50 % cotton fabric, embroidery hoop, white thread, tracing paper, hot-iron transfer pencil, and white vinegar.

1. Unwrap floss and soak for a few minutes in a mixture of 1 cup of water and 1 tablespoon of vinegar. Remove from water and allow to dry.
2. Trace pattern onto tracing paper. Turn pattern over and use transfer pencil to draw over lines of pattern.
3. With transfer pencil side down and edges of pattern ½ " from edges of fabric, pin pattern to one corner of one fabric square. Following manufacturer's instructions, transfer design to fabric.
4. Use 1 strand of floss and Stem Stitch, page 124, to stitch design.
5. Place stitched piece and remaining fabric square right sides together. Using a ¼ " seam allowance and leaving an opening for turning, sew squares together. Cut corners diagonally and turn right side out; press. Sew final closure by hand.

FRUITED CHEESECAKE

Crowned with glazed walnuts and apricots, Fruited Cheesecake gives Christmas fruitcake a fresh, new image. The creamy filling, nestled in a gingersnap crust, features apricots, walnuts, dates, and prunes. For an elegant presentation, place the cake in a foil-wrapped bakery box and tie it with a fancy ribbon. This is one fruitcake your friends will look forward to receiving every year!

FRUITED CHEESECAKE

CHEESECAKE

    1   cup chopped dried apricots, plus
            10 whole dried apricots
    ½   cup brandy
 1 ⅓   cups gingersnap cookie crumbs
    ¼   cup butter or margarine, melted
    ⅔   cup chopped pitted prunes
    ⅔   cup chopped pitted dates
    1   cup coarsely chopped walnuts
    2   tablespoons all-purpose flour
    3   packages (8 ounces each) cream
            cheese, softened
    1   cup granulated sugar
    4   eggs

TOPPING

 1 ½   cups sour cream
    ½   cup apricot preserves, divided
    1   tablespoon brandy
    ⅓   cup coarsely chopped walnuts
    1   tablespoon butter or margarine

Place apricots in a shallow bowl. Add brandy, cover, and soak at room temperature overnight.

Preheat oven to 375 degrees. Line the bottom of a 9-inch springform pan with aluminum foil, wrapping edges under bottom of pan. Combine cookie crumbs and butter. Press into bottom and 1 inch up sides of pan.

Drain apricots, reserving brandy. Set aside whole apricots for garnish. In a medium bowl, combine chopped apricots, prunes, dates, and 1 cup walnuts; toss with flour. In a separate bowl, beat cream cheese until fluffy. Add sugar gradually, mixing well. Add eggs one at a time, beating after each addition. Fold in fruit mixture and reserved brandy. Pour into pan and bake 45 to 50 minutes or until set.

For topping, combine sour cream, 2 tablespoons preserves, and brandy in a small bowl. Spread over cheesecake and bake 5 minutes longer. Allow cake to cool to room temperature. Refrigerate at least 12 hours.

In a small saucepan, melt remaining preserves. Reserving a small amount for garnish, spread preserves over top of cheesecake.

To garnish, sauté walnuts in butter 5 minutes. Drain on a paper towel. Slice reserved whole apricots lengthwise. Remove the side of the springform pan. Use foil lining to gently lift cake from bottom of pan onto a 10-inch dia. piece of cardboard. Referring to photo, arrange apricots and walnuts on top of cake. Glaze with remaining melted preserves.

Yield: 10 to 12 servings

For gift box, follow Gift Box 2 instructions, page 123. We used a 10″ x 10″ x 5½″ cake box purchased from a bakery and decorated it with 1½″ wide satin ribbon.

CHRISTMAS BREAKFAST TREATS

For a sweet Christmas morning surprise, bake up a batch of Santa Danish Rolls! A busy mom will appreciate your ready-to-eat gift because she won't have to cook — and the children will love nibbling the decorated rolls while unwrapping their gifts. You'll like them, too, because they're quick and easy to make with refrigerated breakfast rolls. Fringed fabric makes a festive liner for your gift basket.

SANTA DANISH ROLLS

ROLLS
- 1 package (11 ounces) refrigerated orange Danish rolls
- ¼ cup all-purpose flour
- 1 egg white
- 1 tablespoon cold water
  Red paste food coloring

ICING
- 1⅓ cups confectioners sugar
- 1 egg white
- ⅛ teaspoon cream of tartar
  Licorice, red cinnamon candies, and miniature marshmallows to decorate

Preheat oven to 375 degrees. Unroll each piece of dough and gently brush away cinnamon filling. Sprinkle flour over work area. With lightly floured hands, shape each piece of dough into a ball. Roll lightly in flour. Shape into a smooth oval and place on a greased baking sheet. Pinch top of oval to form a Santa hat. In a small cup, combine egg white, water, and food coloring. Referring to photo, paint hat and cheeks on each roll. Bake 11 to 15 minutes or until lightly browned. Remove from oven. While rolls are still hot, touch up hats and cheeks with colored egg white. Place on wire racks to cool.

For icing, combine sugar, egg white, and cream of tartar in a small bowl and beat until stiff, about 5 minutes. Immediately spoon icing into a pastry bag fitted with a small star tip. For beard and hat trim, refer to photo and pipe icing onto each roll. For face and hat, attach candy pieces and a marshmallow to each roll with icing. Store in airtight container.

Yield: 8 Santa rolls

A CHRISTMAS LIQUEUR

*L*ift holiday spirits with a gift of homemade Coffee Liqueur. For an elegant Christmas offering, present a bottle of the rich liqueur along with a handsomely wrapped box of purchased chocolate liqueur cups. The candy cups will be delicious treats to nibble after sipping the liqueur from them. The flavorful concoction can also be served in coffee or poured over ice cream for a special dessert. A sprig of holly and a tag made of gift wrap and parchment paper add a festive touch.

COFFEE LIQUEUR

6 cups granulated sugar
½ cup instant coffee granules
½ quarts boiling water
1 quart pure grain alcohol
¼ cup vanilla extract

In a large bowl, combine sugar and coffee. Add boiling water, stirring to dissolve. Cool completely. Stir in pure grain alcohol and vanilla. Pour mixture into bottles and close tightly. Let stand in a dark place for at least weeks before serving.

Yield: about 16 cups of liqueur

NORTH POLE DELIVERY

*S*ent special delivery
from the North Pole, here's
a sweet assortment of gifts!
Packaged in tins, baskets,
bags, and jars, the goodies
make an impressive gift for
a family when presented in
a festive crate. The box also
makes a nifty carrier for
delivering small gifts or
holding little surprises
for visitors.

CANDY WREATH ORNAMENTS

3 ½ cups miniature marshmallows
¼ cup butter or margarine
9 large shredded wheat biscuits,
    crushed
½ cup vanilla-flavored candy melts
    or chopped almond bark
Red string candy and red
    cinnamon candies to decorate

In a large saucepan, melt
marshmallows and butter, stirring
until smooth. Stir in crushed biscuits.
To make each wreath, shape ¼ cup
mixture into a small ball. Flatten ball
with palm of hand. Cut out center
with a 1 ½-inch biscuit cutter. Repeat
with remaining mixture. To decorate
with melted candy, follow Kitchen
Tips, page 120. Referring to photo,
drizzle melted candy on wreaths. Tie
string candy in bows. Attach bows and
cinnamon candies with melted candy.
Yield: about 1 ½ dozen wreaths

BUTTERSCOTCH BARS

1 cup all-purpose flour
1 cup quick-cooking rolled oats
¾ cup brown sugar, firmly packed
⅔ cup butter or margarine, melted
½ teaspoon baking soda
¼ teaspoon salt
1 cup butterscotch-flavored baking
    chips
⅔ cup chopped pecans, divided
⅔ cup butterscotch ice cream
    topping
2 tablespoons all-purpose flour

Preheat oven to 350 degrees. In a
large bowl, combine 1 cup flour with
next 5 ingredients. Press two-thirds of
flour mixture into a greased 8-inch
square baking pan. Bake 10 minutes.
Remove from oven and sprinkle with
baking chips and ⅓ cup pecans. In a small
bowl, mix ice cream topping and
2 tablespoons flour; drizzle over
butterscotch chips and pecans.
Sprinkle with remaining flour mixture
and pecans. Bake 15 to 20 minutes or
until lightly browned. Cool completely
before cutting into bars.
Yield: about 2 dozen bars

CREAM SYRUP

2 cups granulated sugar
2 cups light corn syrup
2 cups whipping cream, whipped
1 teaspoon freshly grated nutmeg

In a Dutch oven, combine first
3 ingredients. Bring mixture to a boil;
boil 3 minutes, stirring constantly.
Remove from heat and stir in nutmeg.
Serve warm with French toast,
pancakes, or waffles. Store in airtight
container in refrigerator.
Yield: about 4 cups of syrup

BANANA BUTTER

4 large, ripe bananas, peeled and
    sliced
3 tablespoons lemon juice
1 ½ cups granulated sugar
1 teaspoon pumpkin pie spice

Place bananas and lemon juice in a
blender or food processor fitted with a
steel blade; process until smooth.
Transfer bananas to a large saucepan
and stir in remaining ingredients.
Bring mixture to a boil. Lower heat
and simmer 15 minutes, stirring
frequently. Pour into sterilized jars;
seal. To serve, spread on toast or
English muffins. Store in refrigerator.
Yield: about 3 cups of banana butter

S. CLAUS CRATE

You will need a wooden fruit crate
(we found ours in the produce
department of a grocery store); red,
black, and white acrylic paint;
purchased stickers (ours say "FRAGILE
HANDLE WITH CARE"); paper towels;
Design Master® glossy wood tone
spray; foam brushes; stencil brushes;
Duncan Snow Accents™; and purchased
lettering stencils (we used ½" - 1 ½"h
Roman and Gothic stencils).

1. Paint outside of crate red; allow to dry.
2. Use lettering stencils and follow
Step 2 of How To Stencil, page 122,
to stencil desired phrases on sides of
crate. (We stenciled "PROPERTY OF S.
CLAUS"; "SPECIAL DELIVERY"; and
"FROM: SANTA CLAUS, 12 HOLLY
ROAD, NORTH POLE.")
3. Apply stickers to crate.
4. Lightly spray crate with wood tone
spray; allow to dry.
5. Apply Snow Accents™ to crate along
top edges; allow to dry.

MANY MINI GIFTS

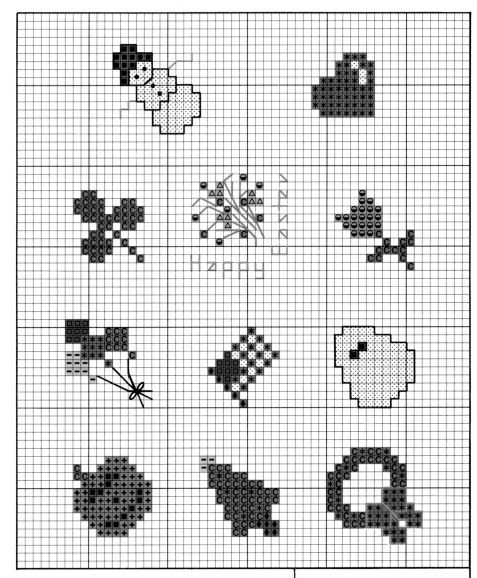

*W*ith this assortment of designs, you can stitch up a mini bread cover any time you need a small gift! Because four little cloths can be cut from one standard bread cover, they're inexpensive and easy to make. For attractive gifts, line miniature market baskets with the cloths and fill them with purchased candies or some of the homemade goodies featured in this book.

MINI BREAD COVERS

You will need White Soft Touch™ (14 ct) Bread Covers (one bread cover will make four mini bread covers) and embroidery floss (see color key).

1. For mini bread covers, match edges and fold bread cover in half; cut along fold. Matching short edges, fold each half of bread cover in half; cut along each fold. To complete fringe, remove 3 fabric threads from cut edges of each mini bread cover.

2. Stitch desired design in one corner of mini bread cover 4 fabric threads from fringe. Use 2 strands of floss for Cross Stitch and 1 for all other stitches. Use 1 strand of floss and Running Stitch (over and under 2 fabric threads) to stitch around mini bread cover 2 fabric threads from fringe.

MINI BREAD COVERS

X	DMC	B'ST	JPC	COLOR
▨	blanc		1001	white
■	310	⟋	8403	black
◉	553	⟋	4097	purple
✚	608		2332	orange
✳	666		3046	red
C	700	⟋	6227	green
–	743		2302	yellow
▣	825		7181	blue
◆	898	⟋	5476	brown
△	957		3125	pink
●	310			black French Knot
⟋	310			black Lazy Daisy

REMEMBERING SPECIAL PEOPLE

Surely great loving-kindness
yet may go with a little gift:
All's dear that comes from friends.

— THEOCRITUS

WELCOME, NEIGHBOR

*M*oving days don't leave much time for cooking, so here's a way to lend a helping hand to new neighbors. Send over a jar of batter for Refrigerator Rolls — your new friends can bake as many as they like. We baked up a few to show you how delicious they look and included the recipe on a fabric-backed card. A basket lined with our reversible buttoned cloth completes this thoughtful housewarming gift.

REFRIGERATOR ROLLS

1 package active dry yeast
2 cups warm water
¾ cup butter or margarine, melted and slightly cooled
¼ cup granulated sugar
1 egg, beaten
4 cups self-rising flour

In a small bowl, dissolve yeast in warm water. In a large bowl, blend butter with sugar. Stir in yeast mixture and egg. Add flour, stirring just until blended. Store covered in refrigerator at least 2 hours before using or up to 5 days.

Yield: batter for 1½ dozen rolls

To bake rolls: Fill greased muffin pan two-thirds full with batter. Cover with a towel and let sit 30 minutes. Bake 20 to 25 minutes at 350 degrees or until lightly browned. If desired, brush with melted butter before serving.

BUTTONED BASKET LINER

You will need a round basket, two coordinating fabrics (amount determined by size of basket), thread to match fabrics, buttons with shanks, and nylon line.

1. To determine diameter of basket liner, measure inside of basket from rim to rim (Fig. 1) and add ½ ". Cut a circle from each fabric the determined diameter.

Fig. 1

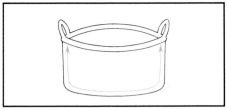

2. With right sides facing and leaving an opening for turning, use a ¼ " seam allowance to sew circles together. Clip seam allowance; turn liner right side out and press. Sew final closure by hand. Topstitch ¼ " from edge of liner.

3. Evenly spacing buttons around basket, use nylon line to attach desired number of buttons to inside o basket near top edge.

4. Referring to Fig. 2 for buttonhole placement and evenly spacing buttonholes around fabric, work one buttonhole on liner for each button o basket.

Fig. 2

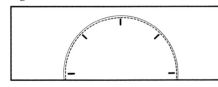

GET-WELL BASKET

This basket of goodies will perk up a friend who's feeling a little under the weather. For an old-time "cure-all" that's filled with nutritious vegetables, tasty chicken, and egg noodles, we prescribed our Cock-A-Noodle Soup. Then we tucked in crackers, lemon drops, a mug with tea bags, and a packet of tissues to round out the surprise. Left at the door as a get-well wish, this offering is sure to lift spirits!

COCK-A-NOODLE SOUP

STOCK

    1 (3½ to 4-pound) chicken
    6 sprigs fresh parsley, stems
          included
    2 onions, quartered
    2 celery stalks, leaves included
    2 bay leaves
    1 turnip, quartered
    1 teaspoon salt
    1 teaspoon black peppercorns,
          crushed
    ½ teaspoon dried thyme

SOUP

    3 quarts stock
    ⅔ cup finely chopped celery
    ½ cup finely chopped carrots
    ½ cup finely chopped onion
    2 teaspoons salt
    ½ teaspoon ground black pepper
    2 cups uncooked thin egg noodles
    3 to 4 cups shredded cooked
          chicken

For stock, place chicken in a Dutch oven with 5 quarts water. Add remaining stock ingredients and bring to a boil. Reduce heat to medium and simmer 30 minutes, skimming foam from the top. Partially cover pan; simmer 30 minutes longer or until juices run clear when chicken is pierced with a fork. Remove chicken and set aside to cool. Add 1 quart water to Dutch oven, partially cover, and simmer 1 hour longer. When chicken has cooled, remove skin and shred meat. Cover and refrigerate until ready to use.

Strain stock through a cheesecloth-lined sieve into a large bowl. Cover and refrigerate at least 8 hours. After refrigerating, skim fat from surface of stock.

For soup, combine 3 quarts stock in large Dutch oven with next 5 ingredients. Bring soup to a boil; cover and reduce heat to low. Cook 30 minutes or until vegetables are tender.

Prepare noodles following package instructions. Add noodles and shredded chicken to soup and simmer 5 minutes.

Yield: about 4 quarts of soup

GARDEN-FRESH BREADS

Our garden-fresh breads are perfect for a friend with a green thumb — or anyone who enjoys the wholesome goodness of vegetables. For a clever presentation that's especially easy, bake the spicy breads in canning jars. Then tuck them in a country basket and add handwritten labels.

CARROT-RAISIN BREAD

    3   cups all-purpose flour
    3   teaspoons caraway seeds
    ¼   teaspoon salt
    1   teaspoon baking soda
 1 ½   teaspoons ground cinnamon
    ¼   teaspoon ground allspice
    ¼   teaspoon ground cloves
 1 ½   cups finely grated carrots
 1 ½   cups raisins
    ⅓   cup butter or margarine,
           softened
    2   cups brown sugar, firmly packed
    2   eggs
    1   cup buttermilk

Preheat oven to 325 degrees. Grease and flour 5 pint-size wide mouth canning jars. In a medium bowl, combine first 9 ingredients, mixing well. In a large bowl, cream butter, sugar, and eggs. Stir in buttermilk. Add flour mixture, stirring just until combined. Fill jars with batter just over half full. Place jars on baking sheet and bake 45 to 50 minutes, testing for doneness with a toothpick. Place jars on a rack to cool.*

Bread may also be baked in two 8 ½ x 4 ½ x 2 ¾ -inch loaf pans 1 hour to 1 hour and 10 minutes at 350 degrees.

Yield: 5 jars or 2 loaves of bread

ZUCCHINI-BRAN BREAD

    3   eggs
    1   cup vegetable oil
    2   cups grated zucchini
    2   cups granulated sugar
    3   teaspoons vanilla extract
    2   cups all-purpose flour
    1   cup whole bran cereal
    3   teaspoons ground cinnamon
    ½   teaspoon salt
    1   teaspoon baking soda
    ¼   teaspoon baking powder
    1   cup chopped walnuts

Preheat oven to 325 degrees. Grease and flour 5 pint-size wide mouth canning jars. In a large bowl, beat eggs and oil until foamy. Add zucchini, sugar, and vanilla, mixing well. In a separate bowl, combine remaining ingredients. Add flour mixture to zucchini mixture, stirring just until combined. Fill jars with batter just over half full. Place jars on baking sheet and bake 40 to 45 minutes, testing for doneness with a toothpick. Place jars on a rack to cool.*

Bread may also be baked in two 8 ½ x 4 ½ x 2 ¾ -inch loaf pans 50 to 60 minutes at 350 degrees.

Yield: 5 jars or 2 loaves of bread

*Note: This is not a canning technique; bread should be eaten fresh or stored in the refrigerator or freezer.

For basket, we lightly brushed grey paint on a white basket and glued artificial ivy to the sides and handle. *For jar lid toppers,* we cut circles of fabric 3″ larger than jar lids and tied them on the lids with jute.

APPLES FOR TEACHER

*S*urprise a beloved teacher with an apple gift basket! The cinnamon-spiced Chunky Applesauce is delicious served warm for dessert or atop pancakes or waffles for a nice breakfast treat. The handcrafted apple makes a charming desk accent. For a cute gift tag, use a paint marker to personalize a miniature wooden book shape.

CHUNKY APPLESAUCE

- 4 pounds cooking apples
- ½ cup water
- ½ cup granulated sugar
- 1 teaspoon ground cinnamon
- ½ teaspoon ground nutmeg
- ¼ teaspoon ground allspice
- ¼ teaspoon ground cloves

Wash, peel, core, and quarter apples. Place in a large Dutch oven with water. Cover and cook 20 to 30 minutes or until apples are tender. Place apples in a blender or food processor fitted with a steel blade. Process briefly, leaving some chunks for texture. Return mixture to Dutch oven. In a small bowl, mix remaining ingredients. Add to apple mixture, blending well. Cook, uncovered, 5 minutes longer.

Yield: about 4½ cups of applesauce

APPLE

You will need a 3″ dia. plastic foam ball, red tissue paper, craft glue, a velvet leaf, and a small twig.

1. Slightly flatten one side (bottom) of foam ball by firmly pressing it on a hard, flat surface.
2. Tear tissue paper into ½″ x 4½″ strips.
3. In a small bowl, mix one part glue to one part water. Dip one strip in glue mixture and pull between fingers to remove excess glue. Place strip on foam ball and smooth wrinkles. Repeat until ball is covered; allow to dry.
4. Repeat Step 3 to apply a second layer of tissue strips to ball.
5. Insert twig and leaf into top of apple; glue to secure.

*H*elp an avid fisherman reel in a sensational supper with a bag of zesty cornmeal coating mix. To serve up his catch of the day, all he has to do is dip the fish in buttermilk and coat it with the mix before frying. He'll love the zing of the lemon pepper seasoning — and he's sure to get a kick out of the easy-to-paint gift bag!

FISH FRY COATING MIX

1 ½   cups yellow cornmeal
¼   cup all-purpose flour
1   tablespoon lemon pepper
2   teaspoons salt
1   teaspoon onion powder
½   teaspoon paprika

In a large bowl, combine all ingredients. Store in an airtight container.

Yield: about 1 ¾ cups of mix

To prepare fried fish: Dip fish in buttermilk and roll in coating mix. To cook, pour oil into a Dutch oven to a depth of 2 to 3 inches. Heat to 375 degrees. Fry coated fish, one piece at a time, about 4 to 6 minutes or until golden brown.

FISH BAG

You will need one 15" square of unbleached muslin; thread to match muslin; tracing paper; flat paintbrush; 13" of ¼" dia. cotton cord; one 1" dia. wooden bead; olive green, black, and rust acrylic paint; black permanent felt-tip pen with fine point; and small pieces of cellulose sponge.

1. Matching arrows to form one pattern, trace fish pattern onto tracing paper. Cut out pattern ½" outside drawn line (stitching line). Use pattern and cut two fish pieces from muslin. Use a pencil to lightly draw mouth and eye on one fish piece (front).
2. Use sponge pieces dipped in black paint to stamp head and body of fish. Use paintbrush to paint eye rust and tail green; allow to dry.
3. Use pen to color mouth and outline eye.
4. Match painted side of fish front piece to remaining fish piece. Using a ½" seam allowance and leaving tail end open, sew fish pieces together. Trim seam allowance and turn fish right side out; press. Press raw edge 1" to wrong side.
5. For closure, knot each end of cord; fold cord in half. Insert folded end of cord through bead. Place loop over fish tail. Place a plastic bag of fish coating mix in fish bag; slide bead toward fish to close bag.

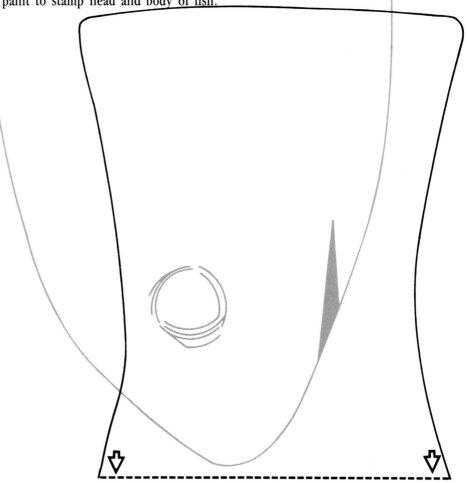

45

A HELPING HAND

W̲hen a friend isn't up to cooking, this hearty Garden Chicken Casserole is a delicious way to lend a helping hand. The wholesome meal, filled with vegetables, rice, chicken, and almonds in a creamy cheese sauce, is sure to be enjoyed by the whole family. The padded carrier is a nice way to deliver the hot dish to your friend in need.

GARDEN CHICKEN CASSEROLE

    2   cups chicken broth
    ⅔   cup sherry, divided
    1   package (6 ounces) long grain
            and wild rice mix
    1   small onion, chopped
    2   small carrots, grated
    1   small green pepper, chopped
    ¼   cup butter or margarine
    3   cups diced cooked chicken
    1   can (4 ounces) sliced mushrooms
    1   package (8 ounces) cream cheese
    2   cups (8 ounces) shredded
            American cheese
    1   cup evaporated milk
    ⅓   cup grated Parmesan cheese
    ½   cup sliced almonds
        Carrots and green onions for
            garnish, optional

In a medium saucepan, bring broth and ⅓ cup sherry to a boil. Add contents of rice package, cover, and simmer over low heat 25 to 30 minutes or until all liquid is absorbed.

Preheat oven to 350 degrees. In a Dutch oven, sauté onion, carrots, and green pepper in butter until soft, about 5 minutes. Add rice, chicken, and mushrooms, mixing well. Place cream cheese, American cheese, and milk in a saucepan and melt over medium heat, stirring until smooth. Add to Dutch oven with remaining sherry, mixing thoroughly. Pour into a buttered 13 x 9 x 2-inch casserole dish. Top with Parmesan cheese and almonds. Cover and bake 35 minutes; uncover and bake 15 minutes longer or until bubbly. If desired, garnish with carrots and green onions.

Yield: about 8 servings

Note: Casserole may be refrigerated overnight before baking. If refrigerated, increase baking time to 45 minutes covered and 15 minutes uncovered.

CASSEROLE CARRIER

You will need two 19½ " x 15½ " pieces of fabric, two 19½ " x 15½ " pieces of craft batting, thread to match fabric, and eight ⅝" dia. buttons.

1. Place batting pieces together. Place fabric pieces right sides together on top of batting pieces. Leaving an opening for turning, use a ½ " seam allowance and stitch all layers together. Turn right side out and press; sew final closure by hand.
2. Stitch 2¾ " from each edge of carrier.
3. Fold fabric up along stitched lines, matching lines to form each corner. Place buttons on both sides of each corner and stitch buttons together to secure.

KEYBOARD COOKIES

KEYBOARD COOKIES

- 24 ounces vanilla-flavored almond bark
- 1 package (8.5 ounces) cream-filled sugar wafer cookies
- 6 ounces chocolate-flavored almond bark

Melt vanilla-flavored almond bark following package instructions. Referring to photo, spread melted almond bark over 12 of the cookies, leaving the upper left corner of each cookie uncoated. Shake gently to remove excess coating and place on a wire rack with waxed paper underneath. Repeat with remaining cookies, leaving the upper right corners uncoated. Cool completely.

Melt chocolate-flavored almond bark following package instructions. With a knife, carefully spread melted candy on the uncoated portion of each cookie to form the ''black keys.'' Return cookies to rack to cool completely.

Yield: about 2 dozen cookies

For gift box, follow Gift Box 1 instructions, page 123. We used a 4¾″ x 14¾″ x ⅞″ tie box and decorated it with ⅝″ wide ribbon.

A sharp gift for a music lover, this edible keyboard is actually made of purchased cookies! We simply coated sugar wafers with vanilla and chocolate almond bark and arranged them in a man's tie box to create a clever piano look-alike. Wrapping paper with a musical note adds harmony to your surprise.

SWEET CONGRATULATIONS

Whether the baby's a boy or a girl, you'll be ready to congratulate the new mother with one of these sweet quick breads! She'll enjoy tangy Blueberry-Lemon Bread (if it's a boy) or delicate Cherry-Almond Bread (if it's a girl). Nestle a freshly baked loaf in a decorated basket along with toys and accessories for the baby, and your gift is sure to be a welcome arrival.

CHERRY-ALMOND BREAD

1 cup granulated sugar
½ cup butter or margarine, softened
2 eggs
2 cups all-purpose flour
1 teaspoon baking soda
½ teaspoon salt
1 cup buttermilk
1 cup chopped almonds
1 jar (10 ounces) maraschino cherries, drained and chopped
1 teaspoon almond extract

Preheat oven to 350 degrees. In a large bowl, cream sugar, butter, and eggs until light and fluffy. In a separate bowl, sift together flour, baking soda, and salt. Blend into creamed mixture with buttermilk. Stir in almonds, cherries, and almond extract. Pour batter into a greased and floured 9 x 5 x 3-inch loaf pan and bake 55 to 60 minutes, testing for doneness with a toothpick. Remove from pan and cool on a wire rack.

Yield: 1 loaf of bread

BLUEBERRY-LEMON BREAD

3 tablespoons shortening
3 tablespoons butter or margarine
1 cup granulated sugar
1 tablespoon grated lemon peel
2 eggs
1 tablespoon fresh lemon juice
1½ cups all-purpose flour
1 teaspoon baking powder
¼ teaspoon salt
½ cup milk
1 cup fresh or frozen blueberries (if frozen, do not thaw)
2 tablespoons all-purpose flour

Preheat oven to 350 degrees. In a large bowl, cream shortening, butter, sugar, and lemon peel. Add eggs and lemon juice, mixing well. In a separate bowl, sift together 1½ cups flour, baking powder, and salt. Blend into creamed mixture with milk. Toss blueberries with 2 tablespoons flour. Gently fold into batter. Pour batter into a greased and floured 9 x 5 x 3-inch loaf pan and bake 50 to 55 minutes, testing for doneness with a toothpick. Remove from pan and cool on a wire rack.

Yield: 1 loaf of bread

BABY BASKETS

For each basket, you will need a basket (we used a half-peck basket), fabric for lining, thread to match fabric, white and desired color acrylic paint, foam brushes, wooden cutouts, craft batting, heavy thread (buttonhole twist), hot glue gun, glue sticks, toothbrush, matte clear acrylic spray, and cardboard.

1. Paint basket white; allow to dry. Paint basket trims, basket handle, and cutouts desired color; allow to dry. Glue cutouts to basket.

2. To spatter white paint, dip toothbrush in paint and pull thumb across top of bristles. Repeat to spatter entire basket; allow to dry. Spray basket with acrylic spray; allow to dry.

3. Determine width of lining fabric by measuring height of basket and adding 6". Determine length of lining fabric by measuring the circumference of the basket at the widest part and multiplying by 2. Cut fabric the determined width and length, piecing if necessary.

4. With right sides facing and using a ½" seam allowance, sew short edges of fabric together. Press seam open.

5. Press one raw edge of fabric 3" to wrong side. Place heavy thread on wrong side of lining 2" from pressed edge; zigzag stitch over heavy thread, being careful not to stitch into thread.

6. Pull heavy thread, evenly gathering fabric to fit inside basket rim; knot thread and trim ends. With 1" of lining extending above top edge of basket, glue fabric along gathering thread to inside of basket.

7. For padded bottom, draw around bottom of basket on cardboard. Cut out cardboard ¼" inside drawn line; place cardboard inside basket and trim to fit. Cut batting same size as cardboard and glue to cardboard.

8. Cut fabric 1½" larger on all sides than cardboard. Using heavy thread, baste around fabric ½" from edge.

9. Center cardboard, batting side down, on wrong side of fabric. Pull ends of basting thread to gather fabric tightly around cardboard; knot thread and trim ends. Straighten folds in lining fabric and glue padded bottom to inside bottom of basket over lining.

AS GOOD AS GOLD

Wrapped in gleaming gold foil, this Gold Bar Candy is a priceless gift for someone who's worth his weight in gold! The easy-to-make bars, molded in ice cube trays, have a rich butter-pecan flavor. And when you deposit the candy in a stenciled "money bag," you'll have a gift that's as good as gold.

GOLD BAR CANDY

- 1 box (3 ½ ounces) vanilla pudding mix (do not use instant)
- 1 cup granulated sugar
- ⅔ cup evaporated milk
- 2 tablespoons butter or margarine
- 1 teaspoon liquid butter flavoring
- ⅔ cup chopped pecans

In a medium saucepan, combine first 3 ingredients. Bring mixture to a boil and continue to boil 5 minutes, stirring constantly. Remove from heat and stir in butter and liquid flavoring. Pour mixture into a medium bowl. Beat with an electric mixer at high speed 4 to 5 minutes or until mixture thickens and is no longer glossy. Stir in pecans. Fill buttered plastic ice cube trays half full with mixture. Refrigerate until firm. Remove candy from trays and wrap in foil candy wrappers. Store in a cool place.

Yield: about 2 dozen candies

MONEY BAG

You will need one 7 ½ " x 22" piece of canvas fabric, thread to match fabric, tagboard (manila folder), tracing paper, graphite transfer paper, craft knife, green acrylic paint, stencil brush, paper towels, 15" of ⅛" dia. cotton cord, two ⅜" dia. gold beads with ⅛" dia. openings, seam ripper, and craft glue.

1. With top of pattern centered 5" from one short edge (top) of fabric, follow How To Stencil, page 122, to stencil dollar sign on fabric.

2. Use fabric and follow Steps 2 and 4 of Fabric Bag instructions, page 122. Press top edge of bag 2" to wrong side.

3. For casing, stitch around top of bag 1 ½ " and 1" from pressed edge. Use seam ripper to open casing on outside of bag at one side seam. Thread cord through casing; glue beads on ends of cord.

FOR THE HOST

What would a ball game be without peanuts! The next time you go to a friend's house to watch the big game, take along some Beer Snack Nuts for your host. The sweet-and-salty nuts are surprisingly easy to prepare — and to present. Just pour them into a decorative beer bottle and tag it with a "baseball" label. Include baseball card coasters featuring his favorite players, and your gift will score a home run!

BEER SNACK NUTS

4½ cups shelled raw peanuts
2 cups granulated sugar
½ teaspoon salt
1 cup water
   Coarse salt

Place peanuts, sugar, ½ teaspoon salt, and water in a Dutch oven and bring to a boil. Continue to boil until all liquid is absorbed, about 25 to 30 minutes.

Preheat oven to 300 degrees. Spread peanuts on a greased 15 x 10 x 1-inch jellyroll pan and sprinkle with coarse salt. Bake 20 minutes. Remove from oven, stir, sprinkle with coarse salt again, and bake 20 minutes longer. Cool completely. Store in airtight container.

Yield: about 4½ cups of nuts

SPORTS COASTERS

For each coaster, you will need one baseball card, one 3¾" square of green mat board, two 6" squares of clear lightweight vinyl (available at fabric stores), one 6" square of white tissue paper, white paint marker, red sewing thread, pinking shears, and craft glue.

1. For baseball diamond, use paint marker to draw a line ¼" from edges of mat board; paint bases and allow to dry. Trim baseball card close to picture; glue card to mat board.
2. Center mat board on one vinyl square; center remaining vinyl square on mat board. Matching edges, place tissue paper square on top.
3. Use zipper foot and stitch all layers together close to mat board; tear away tissue paper. Use pinking shears to trim vinyl ⅜" from stitching.

"Sew" Glad We're Friends

*B*rimming with cookies shaped like buttons and thread spools, this cross-stitched tote bag bears a special message for a stitching friend. The lightly glazed buttery cookies are filled with bits of flavorful almonds. Later, the handy tote will be just right for holding sewing notions.

ALMOND COOKIES

COOKIES

½ cup butter, softened
½ cup margarine, softened
½ cup sifted confectioners sugar
1 egg
½ teaspoon almond extract
2 ½ cups all-purpose flour
½ cup finely chopped almonds, toasted

GLAZE

1 ½ cups sifted confectioners sugar
¼ cup milk
¼ teaspoon almond extract
Purchased pink and blue decorating icing

For cookies, cream butter and margarine in a large bowl. Add sugar, blending until smooth. Add egg and almond extract, beating well. Stir in flour and almonds.

Preheat oven to 350 degrees. With a floured rolling pin, roll out dough on a floured surface to ¼-inch thickness. For spool cookies, trace spool pattern onto tracing paper and cut out. Place spool pattern on dough

and use a paring knife to cut around pattern. For button cookies, cut out dough with a 1-inch dia. bottle cap; use a toothpick to make 2 small holes in center of each cookie. Place on ungreased cookie sheets and bake 8 to 10 minutes or until edges are golden. Cool on wire racks.

For glaze, use a wire whisk to combine first 3 ingredients in a medium bowl. Dip tops of cookies into glaze. Place on wire racks to dry. Referring to photo, decorate spools with decorating icing.

Yield: about 5 dozen cookies

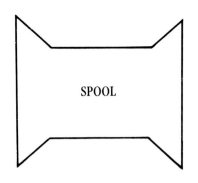

SPOOL

TOTE

You will need one Fiddler's (14 ct) Lil' Tote (6½" x 5") and embroidery floss (see color key).

Work design on tote using 2 strands of floss for Cross Stitch and 1 for Backstitch.

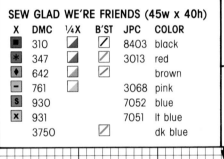

X	DMC	¼X	B'ST	JPC	COLOR
■	310	◨	◨	8403	black
✳	347	◨	◨	3013	red
◆	642	◨	◨		brown
−	761	◨		3068	pink
S	930			7052	blue
x	931			7051	lt blue
	3750		◨		dk blue

SEW GLAD WE'RE FRIENDS (45w x 40h)

Aida 11	4⅛" x 3¾"
Aida 14	3¼" x 2⅞"
Aida 18	2½" x 2¼"
Hardanger 22	2⅛" x 1⅞"

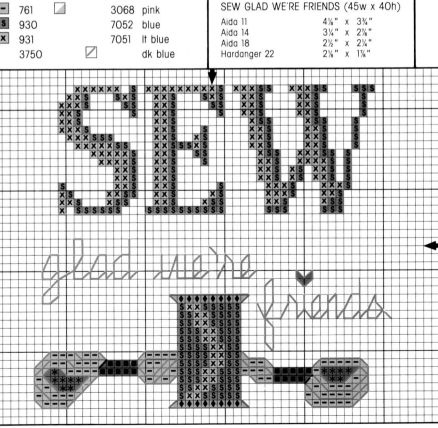

HAPPY BIRTHDAY

NEOPOLITAN DESSERT SPREAD

*S*ay "Happy Birthday" with a parfait glass filled with sweet Neopolitan Dessert Spread! Resembling the popular ice cream, the layered cream cheese spread is flavored with milk chocolate, strawberries, and vanilla. Topped with a dollop of the vanilla-flavored mixture and garnished with sliced strawberries, it's sure to please the party's guest of honor. Include a gift-wrapped box of gingersnaps for serving.

2 packages (8 ounces each) cream cheese, softened
¼ cup confectioners sugar
⅓ cup coarsely chopped strawberries
2 tablespoons chocolate syrup
⅓ cup grated milk chocolate
½ teaspoon vanilla extract
Sliced strawberries for garnish

In a medium bowl, beat cream cheese and sugar until smooth. Divide mixture evenly between 3 small bowls.

Place chopped strawberries between paper towels and press gently to remove excess moisture. Blend strawberries into 1 bowl of cream cheese mixture. Blend syrup and chocolate into second; blend vanilla into third. Referring to photo, layer mixtures into parfait glasses or glass jars, alternating flavors. Garnish with sliced strawberries. Serve with gingersnaps or graham crackers. Store in refrigerator.

Yield: about 2 cups of spread or 2 parfait glasses

54

FOR A "SEASONED" COOK

Experienced cooks know the value of good seasonings. And this pretty sampler of condiments is filled with tantalizing treats they'll love! Our gourmet blends of herbs and spices will add zest to meats and vegetables, and the Lemon Extract is great for baking. To delight a "seasoned" cook, bottle the flavorings in spice jars (found in kitchen accessory shops) and present them in a gift basket with some cheery kitchen towels and an oven mitt.

LEMON EXTRACT

　　1　large lemon
　½　cup vodka

Use a vegetable peeler to remove peel from lemon in small strips, being careful not to include white portion. In a small saucepan, bring lemon peel and vodka to a boil. Remove from heat; pour into a small glass jar and seal. Allow extract to stand at least 2 weeks before using.

Yield: about ½ cup of extract

HERB BLEND

　　3　tablespoons dried whole basil
　　3　tablespoons dried whole
　　　　marjoram
　　3　tablespoons dried whole thyme
　　3　tablespoons dried whole tarragon
　　1　tablespoon dried lemon peel
　　1　tablespoon dried whole oregano

Place all ingredients in a small jar and seal. Shake until mixture is completely blended.

Yield: about ¾ cup of seasoning

SEASONED SALT

　　1　cup salt
　　2　teaspoons granulated sugar
　　2　teaspoons dry mustard
　1 ½　teaspoons dried whole oregano
　1 ½　teaspoons garlic powder
　　1　teaspoon curry powder
　　1　teaspoon onion powder
　½　teaspoon celery seeds
　¼　teaspoon paprika
　¼　teaspoon ground thyme
　⅛　teaspoon ground turmeric

Place all ingredients in a pint jar and seal. Shake until mixture is completely blended.

Yield: about 1 ⅓ cups of seasoning

SEASONED PEPPER

　⅓　cup whole black peppercorns
　　3　tablespoons sweet pepper flakes
　　2　tablespoons whole white
　　　　peppercorns
　　1　teaspoon dried minced onion
　　1　teaspoon crushed red pepper
　　　　flakes
　½　teaspoon dried minced garlic

Place all ingredients in a blender or food processor fitted with a steel blade. Process to a coarse powder. Store in airtight container.

Yield: about ⅔ cup of seasoning

FOR YOUR "MAIN SQUEEZE"

*W*hen it's time to fire up the grill, your "main squeeze" will appreciate a bottle of this hickory-flavored Barbecue Sauce. And he's sure to get a kick out of the clever apron, too! For a sizzling surprise, present the tangy sauce in a squeeze bottle along with the apron and some handy barbecue utensils to use at his next cookout.

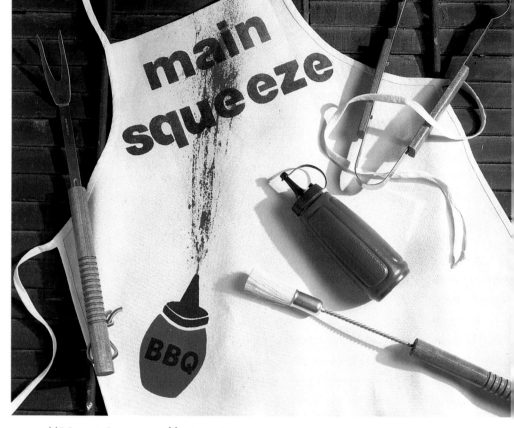

BARBECUE SAUCE

⅓ cup chopped onion
1 tablespoon vegetable oil
1½ cups ketchup
½ cup chili sauce
¼ cup apple cider vinegar
¼ cup molasses
¼ cup steak sauce
3 tablespoons dry mustard
2 tablespoons prepared horseradish
1 teaspoon fresh lemon juice
1 teaspoon liquid barbecue smoke seasoning
1 teaspoon garlic powder
½ teaspoon cayenne pepper
¼ teaspoon ground allspice

In a medium saucepan, sauté onion in oil over medium heat until soft, about 5 minutes. Add remaining ingredients, blending well. Simmer 20 minutes over low heat, stirring frequently. Store in airtight container in refrigerator.

Yield: about 3 cups of sauce

"MAIN SQUEEZE" APRON

You will need a canvas apron; black, dk red, and dk green acrylic paint; lettering stencil (we used a 2"h Helvetica Bold stencil); tagboard (manila folder); paper towels; stencil brushes; craft knife; tracing paper; graphite transfer paper; spray bottle; newspaper; removable tape; and small round paintbrush.

1. Wash, dry, and press apron.
2. (Note: Practice spraying paint on newspaper until desired effect is achieved.) Mix three tablespoons dk red paint to three tablespoons water; pour mixture into spray bottle. Spread newspaper on a flat surface and place apron on top of paper. For "barbecue sauce splatter," lightly spray a single stream of paint across top portion of apron from lower left to upper right; allow to dry.
3. For stenciled container, follow How to Stencil, page 122, to stencil container below sprayed paint at lower left on apron. Allow to dry.
4. Use black paint to paint "BBQ" on stenciled container.
5. Use lettering stencil and follow Step 2 of How to Stencil, page 122, to stencil "main squeeze" on apron. Allow to dry.
6. Heat set design using a hot, dry iron.

FOR THE OUTDOORSMAN

*G*reat for carrying along on hunting or camping trips, our homemade Beef Jerky is a perfect gift for your favorite outdoorsman. He'll enjoy munching on the chewy snacks the next time he's out in the woods. To make the savory treats, just marinate strips of beef overnight and then dry them slowly in the oven. A little camouflage ''hunting boot'' makes a jaunty holder for the jerky.

BEEF JERKY

2 ½ pounds lean round steak
 ⅓ cup soy sauce
 ⅓ cup teriyaki sauce
1 ½ tablespoons liquid barbecue
       smoke seasoning
 ½ teaspoon onion powder
 ½ teaspoon ground black pepper

Place meat in freezer for 2 to 3 hours. Trim all visible fat. Cut meat into long narrow strips, ⅛ to ¼-inch thick.

For marinade, combine remaining ingredients in a small bowl. Place meat slices and marinade in a gallon-size resealable plastic bag or covered, non-metallic container. Seal tightly and refrigerate 8 hours or overnight.

Preheat oven to 150 degrees. Remove meat from marinade and drain on paper towels. Leaving space between each strip, place meat on a wire rack over a foil-lined baking sheet. Bake 10 hours with oven door left ajar. Meat will lose about half of its weight and appear dark brown and dry to the touch. Remove from oven and cool completely. Store in airtight container.

Yield: about 12 ounces of beef jerky

CAMOUFLAGE STOCKING

You will need two 7″ x 11″ pieces of camouflage fabric for stocking, two 7″ x 11″ pieces of fabric for lining, tracing paper, fabric marking pencil, and thread to match fabrics.

1. Matching arrows to form one pattern, trace stocking pattern onto tracing paper and cut out.
2. Leaving top open, use pattern and follow Sewing Shapes, page 122, to make stocking from stocking fabric pieces. Press top edge of stocking ½″ to wrong side.
3. For lining, use lining fabric pieces and repeat Step 2; do not turn right side out.
4. With wrong sides together, insert lining into stocking. Slipstitch lining to stocking.
5. For cuff, fold top edge of stocking 1½″ to outside of stocking.

FOR AN EARLY BIRD

Naturally sweetened with fruit juices, our Sugar-Free Strawberry Spread has a pleasantly tart taste that reflects the true flavor of the berry. It's sure to delight a nature-loving friend, especially when accompanied by a flock of cardinal coasters. Perched in their nest holder, the birds will bring charm to the breakfast table. And the tasty spread will encourage your favorite early bird to linger over breakfast — perhaps while watching some feathered friends feast on scattered bread crumbs in the morning sunshine.

SUGAR-FREE STRAWBERRY SPREAD

1 envelope unflavored gelatin
¼ cup white grape juice
3 cups chopped fresh strawberries
2 tablespoons frozen unsweetened cranberry juice concentrate, thawed
2 tablespoons water
1 tablespoon fresh lemon juice

In a small cup, soften gelatin in grape juice. In a medium saucepan, combine remaining ingredients. Bring mixture to a boil and simmer uncovered 8 minutes, stirring occasionally. Remove from heat and stir in gelatin mixture until dissolved. Cool to room temperature. Store in airtight container in refrigerator.

Yield: about 2 cups of spread

CARDINAL COASTERS

For each coaster, you will need two 7″ squares of red fabric; one 7″ square of craft batting; red thread; yellow, white, and black acrylic paint; small flat paintbrush; tracing paper; small crochet hook (to turn fabric); and removable fabric marking pen.

1. Trace pattern onto tracing paper and cut out.
2. With right sides of fabric squares together, place squares on batting. Follow Sewing Shapes, page 122, to make cardinal, trimming batting close to seam; press. Sew final closure by hand.
3. Topstitch ¼″ from edge of coaster. Stitch along marked line for wing; remove pen line.
4. Referring to pattern, paint beak yellow, face black, and eye white; allow to dry.

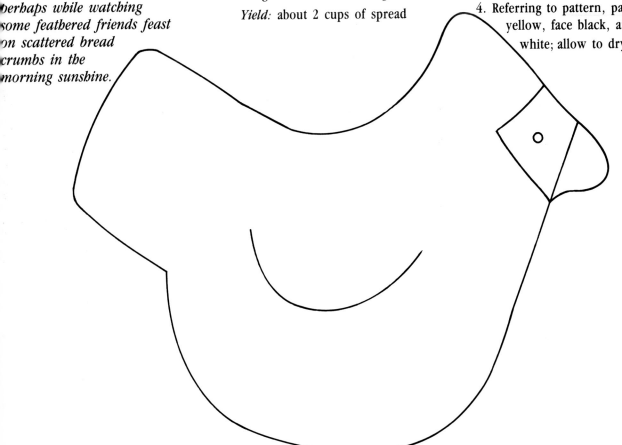

YOU'RE A PEACH

When a friend extends a helping hand, show your appreciation with Peaches and Cream Spread and sweet breads or cookies. The spread is quick to make, so it's perfect for a thank you that just won't wait. A jar topper and basket liner make this a peachy gift!

PEACHES AND CREAM SPREAD

    1   package (8 ounces) cream
        cheese, softened
    ¼   cup confectioners sugar
    3   tablespoons peach preserves
    3   tablespoons peach schnapps or
        peach nectar

In a medium bowl, beat cream cheese until smooth. Add remaining ingredients, blending well. Store in airtight container in refrigerator. Serve with gingersnaps, date nut bread, or favorite quick bread.

Yield: about 1 ¼ cups of spread

PEACHY PROJECTS

You will need a basket; a jar with lid; one 16″ and one 7″ square of unbleached muslin fabric; one 17″ and one 8″ square of print fabric; thread to match fabrics; 25″ of ¼″w ribbon; tagboard (manila folder); craft knife; removable tape; graphite transfer paper; tracing paper; stencil brushes; peach, brown, and green acrylic paint; and paper towels.

1. Stitch ⅝″ from edges of each muslin square; fringe fabric up to stitched lines. Press edges of print fabric squares ¼″ to wrong side; press ¼″ to wrong side again and stitch in place.

2. Following How To Stencil, page 122, center and stencil words along each edge of large muslin square ⅝″ from stitched lines. Stencil peach in corners of large muslin square and in center of small muslin square. Heat set designs by pressing with a hot, dry iron.

3. Place large fabric squares in basket. Place small fabric squares on jar; tie ribbon into a bow around jar lid.

ELEGANCE FOR A SPECIAL SOMEONE

PEANUTTY CHOCOLATES

    1 bar (4 ounces) sweet chocolate
    1 cup peanut butter-flavored
        baking chips
   ½ cup chopped roasted peanuts

Break chocolate into pieces and place in top of a double boiler with baking chips. Melt over medium-low heat, stirring frequently. Remove from heat and spoon into miniature foil cups. Top with chopped peanuts. Refrigerate 30 minutes to set. Store in

*T*here's nothing like an elegantly wrapped gift to make someone feel really special. And with our inexpensive techniques, it's easy to transform an ordinary box into a treasure chest to hold a tasteful treat. Our rich Peanutty Chocolates, nestled in gold foil cups, make a luxurious gift to tuck into such a pretty box.

airtight container in a cool place.

Yield: about 2 dozen candies

For box, follow Gift Box 2 instructions, page 123. We used a 7" x 3⅜" x 2" candy box and decorated it with ⅝" wide metallic ribbon.

YOU'RE "THE CAT'S PAJAMAS"

Here's a gift for a friend who's "the cat's pajamas"! Clad in blue and white striped "pa-jammies," our little kitty is really a simple bag designed to hold a batch of delicious Jammie Muffins. The miniature muffins are topped with a swirl of jam that adds a wonderful fruity taste. After the treats are gone, the cat can be stuffed with fiberfill to make a cuddly accent for the bedroom.

JAMMIE MUFFINS

MUFFINS

1 ½ cups all-purpose flour
⅓ cup granulated sugar
2 teaspoons baking powder
½ teaspoon salt
1 egg, beaten
½ cup milk
¼ cup vegetable oil
1 teaspoon vanilla extract
½ cup desired flavor jam, room temperature

TOPPING

2 tablespoons butter or margarine, melted
¼ cup granulated sugar

Preheat oven to 400 degrees. In a large bowl, combine flour, sugar, baking powder, and salt. In a separate bowl, combine egg, milk, oil, and vanilla. Add to dry ingredients, stirring just until blended. Fill greased miniature muffin pans two-thirds full with batter. Top each with ¼ teaspoon jam. Gently swirl jam into batter with a toothpick. Bake 12 to 15 minutes, testing for doneness with a toothpick. Remove from pans and brush tops with melted butter; sprinkle with sugar. Serve warm.

Yield: about 2 dozen muffins

To reheat: Wrap muffins in aluminum foil and bake in 350 degree oven 10 minutes.

PAJAMA CAT

You will need two 7″ squares and eight 4″ x 9″ pieces of fabric for cat's head and legs; one 10″ x 24″ piece of fabric for pajamas; thread to match fabrics; tracing paper; fabric marking pencil; small crochet hook (to turn fabric); polyester fiberfill; pink, green, and dk grey fabric markers; and ⅔ yd of ⅞″w satin ribbon.

1. Use head and leg patterns and follow Transferring Patterns and Sewing Shapes, page 122, to make one head and four legs from fabric pieces. Stuff shapes with fiberfill and sew final closures by hand.
2. Use dk grey marker to draw facial features and paw pads. Use pink marker to color nose and green marker to color eyes.
3. For pajamas, use fabric and follow Steps 2 - 4 of Fabric Bag instructions, page 122. Whipstitch two legs to bottom of pajamas along fold, placing a leg 1¼″ from each side; whipstitch one leg to each side seam 2½″ from top edge of pajamas.
4. Fold ribbon in half; tack fold to one side seam of pajamas 2″ from top edge. Tack head to top front of pajamas.
5. Place a plastic bag of muffins in pajamas; tie ribbon into a bow around pajamas and trim ends.

HAPPY CAMPER

When you send your child off to summer camp, pack a "survival kit" to help the little camper enjoy the great outdoors. Our yummy Trail Mix, packed in a fun fabric bag, will provide lots of quick energy — and the bag will be great for toting things when the mix is gone. A plastic tackle box makes a sturdy container for the snack bag and other "necessities." We included a canteen, binoculars, a compass, a flashlight, sunglasses, and a utility knife in our kit. To complete your surprise, use felt-tip markers to decorate a poster board tag to match the bag.

TRAIL MIX

     2 cups plain granola cereal
    1½ cups yogurt-covered raisins
     1 cup dry-roasted peanuts
     1 cup dried banana chips
     1 cup dried apple chips
     ⅔ cup chopped dates

Combine all ingredients in a large bowl. Store in airtight container.

Yield: about 7 cups of mix

DRAWSTRING BAG

You will need one 7½" x 22" piece of fabric, thread to match fabric, seam ripper, two 22" lengths of ⅟₁₆" dia. cotton cord, and four ⅜" dia. beads.

1. For bag, use fabric and follow Steps 2 and 4 of Fabric Bag instructions, page 122.
2. For casing, press top edge of bag ¾" to wrong side; stitch ½" from pressed edge. Use seam ripper to open casing on outside of bag at each seamline.
3. For one casing opening, thread one length of cord through entire casing and back out at same opening. Knot ends of cord together 2½" from ends. Thread ends through two beads; knot ends together close to beads. Repeat for remaining casing opening.
4. Place a plastic bag of mix in fabric bag. Pull ends of cords to close bag.

COOKIES FOR MOM

*H*ere's a delicious way to repay Mom for some of those yummy cookies she baked when you were little! Loaded with chocolate chips, nuts, and ground oats, our Favorite Chocolate Chip Cookies are so rich and chewy that she's sure to think they're wonderful. And when you present them along with this cute painted apron, they'll be doubly delightful.

FAVORITE CHOCOLATE CHIP COOKIES

1 cup butter or margarine, softened
1 cup granulated sugar
1 cup brown sugar, firmly packed
2 eggs
1 teaspoon vanilla extract
2 cups all-purpose flour
1 teaspoon baking soda
½ teaspoon salt
2 cups regular rolled oats
1 cup semisweet chocolate chips
1 cup chopped pecans

In a large bowl, cream butter, sugars, eggs, and vanilla until fluffy. In a separate bowl, combine flour, baking soda, and salt. Add to creamed mixture, mixing thoroughly.

Place oats in a blender or food processor fitted with a steel blade; process to the texture of a coarse meal. Stir oats into dough with chocolate chips and pecans. Cover and freeze 1 hour.

Preheat oven to 375 degrees. Shape dough into 1-inch balls and place on ungreased baking sheets. Bake 9 to 12 minutes or until lightly browned around the edges. Allow cookies to cool slightly before removing from baking sheets. Cool on wire racks. Store in airtight container.

Yield: about 6 dozen cookies

APRON

You will need a canvas apron, lt brown and dk brown acrylic paint, stencil brush, tracing paper, graphite transfer paper, tagboard (manila folder), craft knife, paper towels, a 6¼" x 3⅜" x 1" cellulose sponge, foam brush, eight ¼"w black buttons, and black thread.

1. Wash, dry, and press apron.
2. Trace cookie pattern onto tracing paper and cut out.
3. Dampen sponge and squeeze out excess water. Use pattern and cut one cookie from sponge.
4. Use foam brush to apply an even coat of lt brown paint to one side of sponge. Refer to photo to stamp cookie on apron; allow to dry.
5. Use dk brown paint and follow How To Stencil, page 122, to stencil an ''M'' on each side of stamped cookie. Heat set design by pressing with a hot, dry iron.
6. For ''chocolate chips,'' sew buttons to stamped cookie.

A SPECIAL ANNIVERSARY

*H*onor a special
couple on their anniversary
with an elegant decanter of
Italian Cream Liqueur.
Perfect for sipping at
celebrations, the creamy
hazelnut-flavored beverage
is also delicious stirred into
coffee or drizzled over
pound cake. The loving
couple is sure to remember
your thoughtful gift for
years to come.

ITALIAN CREAM LIQUEUR

1 ½ cups whipping cream
1 can (14 ounces) sweetened
    condensed milk
1 cup Frangelico® liqueur
¾ cup vodka
1 teaspoon vanilla extract
½ teaspoon almond extract

Place all ingredients in a blender or
food processor fitted with a steel
blade. Process briefly until completely
blended. Pour into bottles or airtight
container and refrigerate. Serve
chilled.

Yield: about 2 ½ pints of liqueur

Note: Liqueur may be stored in
refrigerator up to 1 month.

FOR AN OLD-FASHIONED FRIEND

A friend who loves the beauty of yesteryear will delight in these softly colored Fruity Macaroon cookies. And since the pretty sweets have only four ingredients, today's cook will find them a pleasure to create. For a special gift, wrap the delicately flavored cookies in a frilly doily and present them in an old-fashioned gift box. A lace-edged tag bearing a hand-lettered message is a dainty finishing touch.

FRUITY MACAROON COOKIES

4 cups flaked coconut
1 can (14 ounces) sweetened condensed milk
½ teaspoon almond extract
1 package (3 ounces) strawberry or other fruit-flavored gelatin

In a large bowl, combine all ingredients. Mix thoroughly, making sure gelatin is blended evenly. Cover and refrigerate at least 2 hours.

Preheat oven to 350 degrees. Shape mixture into 1-inch balls and place on *well-greased* baking sheets. Bake 8 to 10 minutes or until lightly browned around edges. Remove from oven and let cookies cool on baking sheet 5 minutes before placing on wire racks to cool (cookies will be soft).

Yield: about 4 dozen cookies

For tag, write "An Old-fashioned Gift For An Old-fashioned Friend" on a 2" x 3" piece of paper. Glue lace trim around edge of tag.

67

GOOD FOOD, GOOD FRIENDS

68

BUTTERCRUNCH SHORTBREAD

1 cup butter, softened
2 cups sifted all-purpose flour
½ cup sifted confectioners sugar
¼ teaspoon salt
1 (2.1-ounce) Butterfinger® candy
   bar, crushed

Preheat oven to 325 degrees. In a large bowl, cream butter until light and fluffy. In a separate bowl, sift together next 3 ingredients. Blend dry ingredients into butter with crushed candy. Divide dough into 8 pieces; pat into 4½-inch ungreased tart pans. Using a fork, prick the dough in each pan at ½-inch intervals. Bake 18 to 20 minutes or until lightly browned.

Cool completely in pans. Store in airtight container.

Yield: 8 large shortbread cookies

Note: Shortbread may be baked in an ungreased 9-inch square pan. Bake 25 to 30 minutes at 325 degrees; cut into squares while warm.

POTHOLDER

You will need one Ecru Kitchen Mates Potholder (14 ct) and embroidery floss (see color key).

Work design on potholder using 2 strands of floss for Cross Stitch and 1 for Backstitch and French Knots.

*G*ood food and good friends go together, and here's a cookie that's sure to delight a lucky friend! Our Buttercrunch Shortbread is a traditional recipe that we enriched by adding a crushed Butterfinger® candy bar. To give our giant cookie a pretty scalloped border, we baked it in a miniature tart pan. A pocketed potholder, cross stitched with a quilt block pattern and a sweet message, makes an attractive (and useful) carrier for your gift.

GOOD FOOD, GOOD FRIENDS (67w x 67h)

Aida 11	6⅛" x 6⅛"
Aida 14	4⅞" x 4⅞"
Aida 18	3¾" x 3¾"
Hardanger 22	3⅛" x 3⅛"

GOOD FOOD, GOOD FRIENDS (67w x 67h)

X	DMC	B'ST	JPC	COLOR
	898	✓	5476	brown
◉	920		3337	dk rust
✗	922		3336	rust
◯	992		6186	green
•	898			brown French Knot

For The Health Of It

*P*erfect for someone who likes to keep physically fit, our nutty Granola Bars are great energy boosters. The crunchy bars, chock-full of peanuts, sunflower seeds, and granola, make a satisfying treat that's not loaded with sugar. For a power-packed gift, tie a cellophane-wrapped bundle of the snacks with "spring" laces and add it to a basket filled with colorful sports accessories. Your friend will love this gift just "for the health of it"!

GRANOLA BARS

3 ½ cups plain granola cereal
 ½ cup chopped unsalted peanuts
 ¼ cup unsalted sunflower seeds
 ⅓ cup wheat germ
 ¼ cup butter or margarine
 ½ cup brown sugar, firmly packed
 3 tablespoons light corn syrup

Preheat oven to 350 degrees. In a large bowl, combine cereal, peanuts, sunflower seeds, and wheat germ.

In a medium saucepan, melt butter with sugar and corn syrup, stirring constantly until mixture is smooth. Pour over cereal mixture and mix well. Line a 9 x 13 x 2-inch baking pan with aluminum foil. Press granola mixture firmly into pan. Bake 12 to 15 minutes or until lightly browned. Cool completely in pan. Invert pan onto a cutting board; remove foil. Cut into bars with an electric or serrated knife. Store in airtight container.

Yield: about 2 dozen bars

For basket, we threaded shoelaces through the sides of a 7 ½ " x 12" x 4 ½ " wire mesh basket and tied them into a bow on each side.

THINKING OF YOU

*T*opped with sliced *l*monds and a buttery *m*aretto glaze, these moist *tt*le cakes are a luscious *w*ay to say, "I'm thinking *f* you." To deliver your *ift*, cradle one of the cakes *n* a pretty basket that will *ok* nice later in a bedroom *r* bath. To make the tag, *mply* glue flowers cut from *a*bric to a paper card.

UTTERED ALMOND CAKES

AKE

½ cup sliced almonds
½ cup butter or margarine, softened
½ cups granulated sugar, divided
3 egg yolks
½ cups all-purpose flour
¼ teaspoon baking soda
½ cup sour cream
1 teaspoon almond extract
3 egg whites, room temperature

MARETTO GLAZE

6 tablespoons butter or margarine
¼ cup amaretto
¾ cup granulated sugar
2 tablespoons water

Preheat oven to 325 degrees. Grease *d* flour eight 1-cup metal gelatin *ol*ds. Sprinkle almonds in bottoms of *n*s.

In a large bowl, cream butter and *¼* cups sugar. Add egg yolks, one at

a time, beating well after each addition. In a separate bowl, combine flour and baking soda. Add to creamed mixture alternately with sour cream, beginning and ending with flour mixture. Stir in almond extract.

In a medium bowl, beat egg whites until foamy. Add ¼ cup sugar, 1 tablespoon at a time, beating until stiff peaks form. Fold into cake batter. Pour into pans and bake 20 to 25 minutes, testing for doneness with a toothpick. Cool in pans 15 minutes.

While cakes are cooling in pans, combine glaze ingredients in a small saucepan. Boil 4 minutes, stirring constantly. Remove cakes from pans; place on a wire rack with waxed paper spread underneath. While cakes are still warm, use a fork or wooden skewer to poke holes in cakes. Spoon warm glaze over cakes. Allow cakes to

sit at least 4 hours or overnight before serving.

Cake may also be baked in a greased and floured 9 x 5 x 3-inch loaf pan at 325 degrees for 1 hour and 15 minutes, testing for doneness with a toothpick.

Yield: about 8 small cakes or 1 loaf

LACE-TRIMMED BASKET

You will need a basket, 2"w pre-gathered lace trim (amount determined by size of basket), fabric stiffener, craft glue, and ivory spray paint.

1. Following manufacturer's instructions, apply fabric stiffener to lace trim. Remove excess stiffener and place trim around rim of basket; glue to secure. Allow to dry overnight.
2. Spray paint basket; allow to dry.

HEALTHY CHOICES

*N*utrition-minded friends will appreciate these healthy choices! The salad dressing, orangy fruit dip, herb cheese spread, and baked snack chips in our sampling are low-calorie, low-cholesterol treats. For ''high-tech'' nutrition with old-fashioned flair, present the entire collection in a country basket with a ruffled gingham liner. Or if you prefer, give one item and include fresh fruit, vegetables, or crackers to enjoy with it.

HERB YOGURT CHEESE SPREAD

1 carton (32 ounces) plain low-fat
  yogurt (use yogurt without
  added gelatin)
3 tablespoons reduced-calorie
  mayonnaise
1 clove garlic, minced
¼ cup minced green onion
1 tablespoon chopped fresh parsley
1 teaspoon Worcestershire sauce
¼ teaspoon salt
⅛ teaspoon ground black pepper
⅛ teaspoon cayenne pepper

To make yogurt cheese, place a
colander over a large glass or ceramic
bowl. Line colander with 4 layers of
cheesecloth; spoon yogurt into
colander. Cover with plastic wrap and
refrigerate 12 hours to drain. Spoon
yogurt cheese into an airtight
container; discard cheesecloth and
drained liquid. (You should have about
2 cups of cheese.)

To make Herb Yogurt Cheese
Spread, combine 1 cup yogurt cheese
with remaining ingredients in a small
bowl. Stir well to blend (do not beat
or use a food processor). Cover and
refrigerate 8 hours or overnight. Serve
with crackers or fresh vegetables.
Store in airtight container in
refrigerator.

Yield: about 1½ cups of spread;
5 calories per tablespoon

Note: Use remaining yogurt cheese as
a low-calorie substitute for sour
cream. If cooking with yogurt cheese,
bring to room temperature before
adding to hot mixtures.

SKINNY FRUIT DIP

1 cup low-fat cottage cheese
3 tablespoons plain low-fat yogurt
2½ tablespoons low-sugar orange
  marmalade
1 tablespoon orange juice
2 teaspoons honey

Place all ingredients in a blender or
food processor fitted with a steel
blade. Process until smooth and
creamy. Serve with fresh fruit. Store
in airtight container in refrigerator.

Yield: about 1⅓ cups of dip;
14 calories per tablespoon

DIET THOUSAND ISLAND DRESSING

1 cup reduced-calorie mayonnaise
⅔ cup spicy vegetable juice
3 tablespoons sweet pickle relish
1 tablespoon minced onion
1 tablespoon minced green pepper
¼ teaspoon dry mustard
⅛ teaspoon garlic powder
⅛ teaspoon ground black pepper

In a medium bowl, use a wire
whisk to blend all ingredients. Cover
and refrigerate at least 2 hours before
serving. Store in airtight container in
refrigerator.

Yield: about 2 cups of dressing;
25 calories per tablespoon

GUILT-FREE SNACK CHIPS

1 package (10 ounces) flour
  tortillas
¼ cup low-calorie Italian salad
  dressing
  Garlic salt or salt-free herb and
  spice blend

Preheat oven to 325 degrees. Cut
each tortilla into eighths. Spread on a
baking sheet lightly sprayed with
cooking spray. Using a pastry brush,
brush salad dressing over tops of
chips. Sprinkle with garlic salt or herb
blend. Bake 10 to 12 minutes or until
lightly browned. Cool completely
before storing in airtight container.

Yield: about 7 cups of chips;
10 calories per chip

RUFFLED BASKET LINER

You will need two 17" squares of
fabric, one 5" x 136" strip of fabric
for ruffle (pieced as necessary), and
thread to match fabric.

1. For ruffle, press short edges of
fabric strip ½" to wrong side. With
wrong sides together, fold fabric in
half lengthwise; press. Baste ⅜" and
¼" from raw edge. Pull basting
threads, drawing up gathers to fit
around fabric square.
2. Matching raw edges and overlapping
ends of ruffle, baste ruffle to right
side of one fabric square.
3. Matching right sides and raw edges,
place fabric squares together. Leaving
an opening for turning, use a ½"
seam allowance and sew fabric squares
together. Cut corners diagonally and
turn right side out; press. Sew final
closure by hand.

store-bought

GIVING SPECIAL GIFTS

Every gift which is given,
even though it be small,
is in reality great,
if it be given with affection.

— PINDAR

IT'S A BO

IT'S A GIRL!

2 CUPS CRUST
TIL A SOFT DOUGH
STROKES.
GREASED 12 INCH
UP GRATED PAR-
SAUCE OVER DOUGH.
D MOZZARELLA
TOPPINGS. BAKE FOR
ES ARE CRISP.

SAUCY ACCENTS

*L*ight and airy, our Mustard Mousse Sauce is a delectably different condiment to serve with ham or roast pork. Since the sauce is made for pork, why not sponge-paint a pottery piggy bank to give with it! After the sauce is all gone, the bank will make a cute kitchen accent and be a reminder of your thoughtfulness. To deliver your gift, pen up the saucy pair in a little wooden crate.

MUSTARD MOUSSE SAUCE

      2 egg yolks, room temperature
      1 clove garlic, minced
      2 teaspoons Dijon mustard
      1 tablespoon sherry vinegar
      1 teaspoon dry mustard
      1 teaspoon honey
    ½ teaspoon salt
    ⅛ teaspoon cayenne pepper
    ⅛ teaspoon ground nutmeg
      1 cup vegetable oil
      3 tablespoons sour cream
    ½ cup whipping cream, whipped

Place first 9 ingredients in a blender or food processor fitted with a steel blade. Process until smooth. With machine running, slowly pour oil into mixture. Continue processing until mixture thickens to the consistency of mayonnaise. Pour mixture into a medium bowl. Gently fold in remaining ingredients. Serve chilled with baked ham. Store in airtight container in refrigerator.

Yield: 2 cups of sauce

PIGGY BANK

You will need one pottery or ceramic piggy bank (we bought ours at a Mexican restaurant), gesso, cream and blue acrylic paint, foam brush, cellulose sponge, glossy clear acrylic spray, and tracing paper.

1. Apply two coats of gesso, then two coats of cream paint to bank, allowing to dry between coats.
2. Trace ring pattern onto tracing paper and cut out.
3. Dampen sponge and squeeze out excess water. Use pattern and cut one ring from sponge.
4. Use foam brush to apply an even coat of blue paint to one side of sponge. Reapplying paint after each stamp and slightly overlapping rings, stamp bank; allow to dry.
5. Spray bank with acrylic spray; allow to dry.

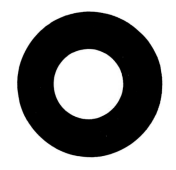

REUBEN SPREAD

*G*ive a bit of Olde World cheer with a German beer stein filled with hearty Reuben Spread. Loaded with corned beef, Swiss cheese, and sauerkraut, the tasty spread combines all the makings of the popular sandwich with a delicious cream cheese base! For serving, include a basket of miniature rye bread slices or crackers. A tag inscribed with "gemütlichkeit," the German word for friendship and camaraderie, imparts warm feelings.

REUBEN SPREAD

  1 package (8 ounces) cream cheese, softened

  ¼ cup seafood cocktail sauce

  1 cup (4 ounces) grated Swiss cheese

  ¼ pound deli corned beef, finely chopped

  ¾ cup sauerkraut, drained and chopped

In a medium bowl, combine cream cheese and cocktail sauce, mixing until smooth. Add remaining ingredients, blending thoroughly. Store in airtight container in refrigerator. Serve with cocktail rye bread slices or rye crackers.

Yield: about 2 ½ cups of spread

SOUTH OF THE BORDER

*S*end someone south of the border with a batch of spicy Chili Con Queso Dip! Created with our own blend of cheese, tomatoes, chilies, and spices, the dip is enhanced with the smoky flavor of bacon. Include a bag of chips and a hot pad stenciled with chili peppers for a red-hot gift.

CHILI CON QUESO DIP

2   slices bacon, chopped
2   tablespoons chopped onion
1   clove garlic, minced
1   can (14.5 ounces) whole tomatoes, undrained
1   can (4 ounces) chopped green chilies
1   teaspoon ground cumin
½   teaspoon salt
½   teaspoon dried whole oregano
¼   teaspoon ground black pepper
4   cups (16 ounces) grated American cheese

In a large saucepan, cook bacon until crisp. Add onion and garlic and cook until onion is soft, about 5 minutes. Stir in next 6 ingredients, blending well. Reduce heat to low and gradually add cheese, stirring until melted. Serve hot with tortilla or corn chips.

Yield: about 4 cups of dip

CHILI PEPPER PROJECTS

You will need two 7½" squares of unbleached muslin fabric; four 2" x 8½" pieces of green fabric for binding; green thread; two 7½" squares of craft batting; tagboard (manila folder); tracing paper; graphite transfer paper; craft knife; removable tape; red, yellow, and green acrylic paint; stencil brushes; paper towels; brown paper bag; hole punch; and green raffia.

1. (Note: For red pepper stencil, use pattern as shown. For yellow pepper stencil, turn pattern over and cut out stencil in reverse.) For hot pad, follow How To Stencil, page 122, to stencil peppers on one muslin square. Heat set design by pressing with a hot, dry iron.

2. Matching edges, place batting squares on remaining muslin square; place stenciled muslin square right side up on batting. Baste all layers together.
3. (Note: Use a ½" seam allowance.) To bind edges of hot pad, press short edges and one long edge of each binding strip ½" to wrong side. With right sides together and matching raw edges, sew one strip to one edge of hot pad. Fold binding over raw edge of hot pad to back; whipstitch pressed edge in place. Repeat for remaining edges. Remove basting threads.
4. For paper bag, repeat Step 1 to stencil peppers on one side of bag; do not heat set.
5. Place a plastic bag of chips in paper bag. Fold top of bag to back. Punch two holes near top fold of bag; thread raffia through holes and tie into a bow.

BAGEL BAGS

*S*easeoned with onion or garlic, our crispy Bagel Snack Chips are easy and inexpensive to make. Your favorite snacker is sure to enjoy a bag (or two!) of these chips. For quick-to-make packages, stitch up some colorful cellophane bags on your sewing machine. Cleverly painted shapes glued to clothespins make cute closures.

BAGEL SNACK CHIPS

- 6 plain bagels
- 6 tablespoons butter or margarine, softened
- 3 teaspoons garlic or onion salt

Refrigerate bagels at least 1 hour for easier slicing. Preheat oven to 325 degrees. To slice bagel, place bagel flat on cutting board. With a serrated knife, cut bagel in half vertically. Place halves on cutting board, cut side down. Cut halves into thin slices, about ¼-inch thick. Repeat with remaining bagels. Place slices on ungreased baking sheets.

In a small bowl, blend butter with garlic or onion salt. Spread over tops of slices and bake 15 to 20 minutes or until lightly browned. Cool on a wire rack. Store in airtight container.

Yield: about 14 cups of chips

CELLOPHANE BAGS

For each bag, you will need colored cellophane, pinking shears, thread to match cellophane, and one 6″ x 10″ piece of tissue paper.

1. Use pinking shears to cut a 6″ x 20″ piece of cellophane.
2. Matching short edges (top), fold cellophane in half. Matching edges, place cellophane on tissue paper. Using a ¼″ seam allowance, sew through all layers along sides of bag; carefully tear away tissue paper.

For tags, paint 1⅛″w wooden heart cutouts and write "Onion" and "Garlic" on them with a permanent felt-tip pen. Glue ⅛″w satin ribbons to the top of the onion tag. Glue a small piece of jute to the bottom of the garlic tag and unravel it. Glue the tags to miniature clothespins.

This Caribbean Cooler Punch will make your friends feel like they've spent a day at the beach — even if they've stayed in their own backyard! A sparkling blend of peach nectar, orange and pineapple juices, and light rum, the fruity drink has tropical appeal. It can also be made without rum for a nonalcoholic refreshment. To present the punch, pour it into a jar with a spigot for easy refills and include a set of playful glasses.

CARIBBEAN COOLER PUNCH

2 ½ cups peach nectar
  2 cups orange juice
  1 cup pineapple juice
1 ½ cups light rum
  1 cup club soda
  ½ cup granulated sugar
  2 teaspoons grenadine

Combine all ingredients in a 2-quart pitcher. Serve chilled or over ice. Store in refrigerator.

Yield: about 2 quarts of punch

*S*omeone who likes to curl up with a good cup of coffee will savor one of our gourmet blends. To create exquisite flavors in your own kitchen, simply add spices and extracts to ordinary ground coffee. Coated paper bags from a gourmet coffee shop are an inexpensive way to pack the coffee. For an extra thoughtful gift, slip the bag of coffee into a basket with a mug and some treats. Sticks of cinnamon or candy make flavorful stirrers, and little candies can be dropped in the coffee to enhance the taste.

BRANDIED SPICE COFFEE

⅓ cup ground coffee
½ teaspoon brandy extract
1 ½ (3 or 4-inch) cinnamon sticks
¼ teaspoon whole cloves
¼ teaspoon whole allspice

Place coffee in a blender or food processor fitted with a steel blade. With processor running, add brandy extract. Stop and scrape sides of container with a spatula. Process 10 seconds longer. Place mix in a small bowl and add remaining ingredients. Store in refrigerator.

Yield: mix for eight 6-ounce servings

CHOCOLATE-MINT COFFEE

⅓ cup ground coffee
1 teaspoon chocolate extract
½ teaspoon mint extract
¼ teaspoon vanilla extract

Place coffee in a blender or food processor fitted with a steel blade. In a cup, combine extracts. With processor running, add extracts. Stop and scrape sides of container with a spatula. Process 10 seconds longer. Store in refrigerator.

Yield: mix for eight 6-ounce servings

BUTTERED RUM COFFEE

⅓ cup ground coffee
¼ teaspoon freshly ground nutmeg
1 ¼ teaspoons rum extract
⅛ teaspoon liquid butter flavoring

Place coffee and nutmeg in a blender or food processor fitted with a steel blade. In a cup, combine remaining ingredients. With processor running, add flavorings. Stop processor and scrape sides of container with a spatula. Process 10 seconds longer. Store in refrigerator.

Yield: mix for eight 6-ounce servings

VANILLA-ALMOND COFFEE

⅓ cup ground coffee
1 teaspoon vanilla extract
½ teaspoon almond extract
¼ teaspoon anise seeds

Place coffee in a blender or food processor fitted with a steel blade. In a cup, combine remaining ingredients. With processor running, add flavorings. Stop and scrape sides of container with a spatula. Process 10 seconds longer. Store in refrigerator.

Yield: mix for eight 6-ounce servings

ORANGE-CINNAMON COFFEE

⅓ cup ground coffee
1 tablespoon grated orange peel
½ teaspoon vanilla extract
1 ½ (3 or 4-inch) cinnamon sticks

Place coffee and orange peel in a blender or food processor fitted with a steel blade. With processor running, add vanilla. Stop and scrape sides of container with a spatula. Process 10 seconds longer. Place mix in a small bowl and stir in cinnamon sticks. Store in refrigerator.

Yield: mix for eight 6-ounce servings

CHOCOLATE-ALMOND COFFEE

⅓ cup ground coffee
¼ teaspoon freshly ground nutmeg
½ teaspoon chocolate extract
½ teaspoon almond extract
¼ cup toasted almonds, chopped

Place coffee and nutmeg in a blender or food processor fitted with a steel blade. With processor running, add extracts. Stop and scrape sides of container with a spatula. Process 10 seconds longer. Place mix in a bowl and stir in almonds. Store in refrigerator.

Yield: mix for eight 6-ounce servings

Brewing instructions: Place mix in filter of an automatic drip coffee maker. Add 6 cups water and brew.

PIZZA-TO-GO

*P*acked with all the makings for delicious homemade pizza, this basket will add pizzazz to a special friend's day. To make it, tuck a jar of our chunky Pizza Sauce and a bag of Crust Mix into a basket filled with an assortment of fresh toppings. And don't forget to include the recipe! A set of red, white, and green napkins, the colors of Italy's flag, adds Continental flair.

PIZZA SAUCE AND CRUST MIX

- 2 large ripe tomatoes, peeled, seeded, and quartered
- 1 cup tomato sauce
- ⅓ cup tomato paste
- 2 teaspoons Italian seasoning
- 1 teaspoon garlic salt
- 1 teaspoon granulated sugar
- ¼ teaspoon ground black pepper
- 4 cups biscuit baking mix

For sauce, use a blender or food processor fitted with a steel blade to coarsely chop tomatoes. Transfer tomatoes to a mixing bowl. Place remaining ingredients, except baking mix, in processor; blend until smooth. Add to tomatoes, mixing well. Cover and store in refrigerator.

For crust mix, place biscuit mix in a resealable plastic bag. Give Pizza Sauce and Crust Mix with recipe for Pizza.

Yield: about 2 cups of sauce and 4 cups of crust mix, enough for two 12-inch pizzas

PIZZA

- 2 cups Crust Mix
- ½ cup cold water
- ½ cup grated Parmesan cheese
- 1 cup Pizza Sauce
- 1½ cups (6 ounces) grated mozzarella cheese
- ¼ pound pepperoni, sliced
  Chopped green pepper, onion, olives, and mushrooms

Preheat oven to 425 degrees. In a medium bowl, combine Crust Mix with cold water. Beat with a wooden spoon about 20 strokes. Pat dough into a greased 12-inch pizza pan. Sprinkle with Parmesan cheese. Spread with Pizza Sauce and top with remaining ingredients. Bake 20 to 25 minutes or until crisp around the edges.

Yield: one 12-inch pizza

For crust mix bag, use a 7½" x 25" piece of fabric and follow Steps 2 and 3 of Fabric Bag instructions, page 122. Place plastic bag of crust mix in fabric bag; tie a ribbon into a bow around bag.

SALAD SPRINKLES

*H*elp a friend add flair to an ordinary salad with these seasoned Salad Sprinkles. This crunchy mixture is a blend of shoestring potatoes, sunflower and sesame seeds, and bacon bits. Our ladybug box is a cute way to present it, especially when nestled in a basket of fresh or silk salad greens.

SALAD SPRINKLES

⅔ cup shoestring potato sticks
½ cup roasted sunflower seeds
2 tablespoons imitation bacon bits
2 tablespoons salad seasoning
   (in grocery spice section)
2 tablespoons sesame seeds
1 teaspoon Italian seasoning
½ teaspoon seasoned pepper

Break potato sticks into small pieces. Combine with remaining ingredients in a small bowl. To serve, sprinkle generously over green salads. Store in airtight container.

Yield: about 1½ cups of sprinkles

LADYBUG BOX

You will need an oval Shaker box (we used a 3½" x 5" box); red, black, and white acrylic paint; desired paintbrushes; and glossy clear acrylic spray.

1. Referring to photo, use a pencil to lightly draw outlines of design on box and lid.
2. Use red and black paint to paint design on box and lid. Use white paint and wooden end of paintbrush to paint dots for eyes; allow to dry.
3. Apply two coats of acrylic spray to box and lid, allowing to dry between coats.

With this tasty trio of snacks, it's easy to please the whole family! For Papa Bear, there's Crispy Snack Mix, a salty blend of cashews, sesame sticks, and chow mein noodles. Mama Bear will enjoy pecan-filled Meringue Snack Mix, and little bears will really go for chocolaty Peanut Butter Snack Mix. Deliver the treats in jars labeled with Mama, Papa, and Baby Bear silhouettes, and your gift is sure to be "not too hot, not too cold, but just right" for everyone.

MERINGUE SNACK MIX

      3 cups miniature saltine crackers
   1 ½ cups pecan halves
      3 egg whites
      1 cup granulated sugar
      1 teaspoon vanilla extract

Preheat oven to 300 degrees. In a large bowl, combine crackers and pecans. In a medium bowl, beat egg whites until stiff. Add sugar and vanilla, mixing well. Fold mixture into crackers and pecans, stirring to coat completely. Spread mixture on a well-buttered baking sheet. Bake 20 minutes, stirring after 10 minutes. Spread mix on waxed paper to cool completely. Break into pieces and store in airtight container.

Yield: about 10 cups of mix

PEANUT BUTTER SNACK MIX

   10 cups rice square cereal
      1 package (12 ounces) semisweet
            chocolate chips
   1 ¾ cups smooth peanut butter
      ½ cup butter or margarine, melted
   3 ½ cups confectioners sugar, sifted

Place cereal in a large bowl. In a medium saucepan, melt chocolate chips over low heat. Add peanut butter and butter, stirring until smooth. Remove from heat and pour over cereal, stirring to coat completely. Pour mixture into a large brown paper bag. Add 1 cup sugar to bag and stir. Close bag securely and shake briefly. Repeat with remaining sugar, adding 1 cup at a time. Spread mix on waxed paper and cool 1 hour or until chocolate is no longer soft. Store in airtight container.

Yield: about 13 cups of mix

CRISPY SNACK MIX

   2 ½ cups chow mein noodles
   1 ½ cups sesame snack sticks
   1 ½ cups salted cashews
      ¼ cup butter or margarine, melted
      ¼ cup soy sauce
   1 ½ teaspoons garlic salt

Preheat oven to 200 degrees. In a large bowl, combine first 3 ingredients. In a small bowl, combine butter, soy sauce, and garlic salt. Pour over snack mixture, stirring to coat. Spread mix on a buttered baking sheet and bake 15 minutes, stirring every 5 minutes. Cool and store in airtight container.

Yield: about 5 ½ cups of mix

THREE BEARS JARS

You will need three jars (graduated in size); black silhouette paper for scherenschnitte; dollhouse wallpaper or paper with a small print; small, sharp scissors; tracing paper; graphite transfer paper; spray adhesive; white acrylic paint; small round paintbrush; black paint pen with fine point; 27" of ¼"w black ribbon; black felt-tip pen with fine point; hot glue gun; and glue sticks.

1. Trace bear patterns onto tracing paper. Use transfer paper to transfer patterns to wrong side (white side) of silhouette paper. Cut out bears.
2. For silhouettes, apply spray adhesive to wrong sides of bears. Place bears, adhesive side down, on wallpaper and press firmly to secure. Cut out wallpaper along outer edges of silhouettes.
3. Use white paint to paint bow tie on Papa Bear, bow and pearls on Mama Bear, and collar and buttons on Baby Bear. Allow to dry. Use felt-tip pen to draw wisps of hair and bow on Baby Bear; allow to dry.
4. Apply spray adhesive to wrong sides of silhouettes. Place silhouettes in desired positions on jars and press firmly to secure. Use paint pen to draw lines for hangers on jars; allow to dry.
5. Cut three 9" lengths of ribbon. Tie each length into a bow. Glue bows to jars at tops of hanger lines.

A PERFECT MATCH

Unique containers for your food gifts are everywhere! Whether found at antique shops or garage sales, decorative jars, tins, boxes, or dishes can make extra-special packaging for your home-cooked creations. Just use your imagination to match them up. We found this blue glass chicken at a local flea market and thought it would be a perfect match for our spicy Chicken Chutney Salad! Filled with juicy pineapple, tender chicken, and crunchy celery, the tropical salad is enhanced with curry powder and sweet chutney. Toasted almonds lend delicious texture to the dish. The lucky recipient can serve the salad on a nest of crisp lettuce leaves for a light, tasty meal.

CHICKEN CHUTNEY SALAD

3 cups diced cooked chicken
1 cup canned pineapple chunks, drained with juice reserved
¾ cup sliced celery
½ cup mayonnaise
¼ cup sour cream
3 tablespoons prepared chutney
1 teaspoon curry powder
½ cup slivered almonds, toasted

In a large bowl, combine chicken, pineapple, and celery. In a separate bowl, use a wire whisk to blend 3 tablespoons reserved juice with remaining ingredients, except almonds. Stir into chicken mixture. Cover and refrigerate at least 1 hour. Stir in almonds before serving. If desired, serve on lettuce leaves.

Yield: about 4 to 6 servings

BLUE PAIL SPECIAL

A *delicious twist on the traditional spread, our Pimiento Jack Cheese is perfect for a picnic or sack lunch. Spanish olives offer a tangy contrast to mild Monterey Jack cheese and sweet pimiento peppers, giving the spread a unique flavor. Our special blue pail, lined with checkered napkins, makes a charming carrier. Later, this little "graniteware" bucket will lend an old-timey look to a country kitchen.*

PIMIENTO JACK CHEESE

- 4 cups (1 pound) grated Monterey Jack cheese
- 1 jar (4 ounces) chopped pimiento, drained
- ½ cup sliced pimiento-stuffed olives
- 3 tablespoons grated onion
- ½ cup mayonnaise
- 3 tablespoons milk
- 1 teaspoon Dijon mustard
- ¼ teaspoon ground white pepper

In a large bowl, combine cheese, pimiento, olives, and onion. In a small bowl, blend mayonnaise, milk, mustard, and pepper until smooth. Add to cheese mixture, mixing well. Store in airtight container in refrigerator. Serve with bread or crackers.

Yield: 3 cups of spread

"GRANITEWARE" PAIL

You will need a small metal pail (we bought our 1 qt. pail at a paint store), blue spray paint, white acrylic paint, plastic fork, and matte clear acrylic spray.

1. Spray pail with a light coat of blue paint; allow to dry. Repeat until pail is evenly coated with paint.
2. Use fork dipped in white paint to paint dots; allow to dry.
3. Spray pail with acrylic spray; allow to dry.

PRIVATE LABELS

PRIVATE LABELS

Whether tied to baskets, pasted on paper bags, or glued to jars and bottles, your own private labels will add a personal touch to all your food gifts. And with our designs and easy photocopying instructions, creating them is fun! Use the labels with your original recipes or any of ours, like this Nutty Herb Rice Seasoning.

For each label, you will need desired rub-on lettering (we used ⅛" - ⅜" high letters); small, sharp scissors; burnisher (available at art supply stores) or small crochet hook; and removable tape and photo to fit in label opening (optional).

1. Make a photocopy of desired label, on this page or page 92, on white paper. Do not cut out.
2. Use a ruler to draw a straight line on another piece of white paper.
3. Place photocopy on top of paper with drawn line. Using line as a guide to keep letters straight, use tip of burnisher or crochet hook to rub letters onto photocopy to form desired words.
4. For label with photo, cut out oval or heart opening. Tape photo to back of photocopy behind cutout area.
5. Make photocopies of completed label on desired color paper; cut out label along outer edges.

NUTTY HERB RICE SEASONING

   1   cup slivered almonds
   ½   cup instant chicken bouillon
   ½   cup dried parsley
   1   tablespoon dried whole basil
   1   tablespoon dried minced onion
   1   tablespoon dried dill weed
   2   teaspoons seasoned salt
   1   teaspoon garlic powder
   ½   teaspoon dried lemon peel
   ½   teaspoon ground black pepper

Place all ingredients in a resealable plastic bag or jar; seal and shake to mix.

Yield: about 2 cups of seasoning

To make rice: Combine 1 cup uncooked rice, 2 cups water, 3 tablespoons seasoning, and 1 tablespoon butter or margarine in a medium saucepan. Bring to a boil, cover, and reduce heat to low. Cook 20 to 25 minutes or until all liquid is absorbed.

Continued on page 92

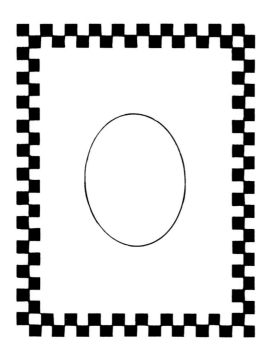

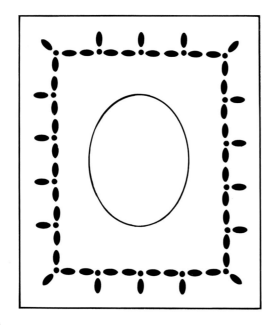

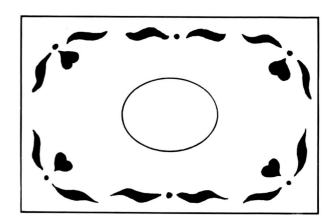

LEMON DELIGHT

Give a little taste of sunshine with zesty Lemon Tea Mix! A refreshing twist on hot spiced tea, our special blend features crushed lemon drop candies. Packed in a brightly painted "lemon" box, the tea will bring a delightful ray of cheer to any day.

LEMON TEA MIX

½ cup instant tea
½ cup sweetened lemonade
    drink mix
¼ cup brown sugar, firmly packed
¼ cup finely crushed lemon
    drop candies

Place all ingredients in a blender or food processor fitted with a steel blade. Process briefly until ingredients are completely blended. Store in airtight container.

Yield: about 1½ cups of mix

To serve: Add 1 cup boiling water to 1 heaping tablespoon tea mix. Stir until mix dissolves completely.

LEMON BOX

You will need one 4″ dia. Shaker box; tracing paper; graphite transfer paper; dk yellow, yellow, lt yellow, and gold acrylic paint; desired paintbrushes; and glossy clear acrylic spray.

1. Use pattern and follow Transferring Patterns, page 122. Use transfer paper to transfer pattern to box lid.
2. Paint lid using dk yellow for rind, lt yellow for membrane, yellow for pulp, and gold for seeds; allow to dry.
3. Paint box and side of lid dk yellow; allow to dry.
4. Apply two coats of acrylic spray to box and lid, allowing to dry between coats.

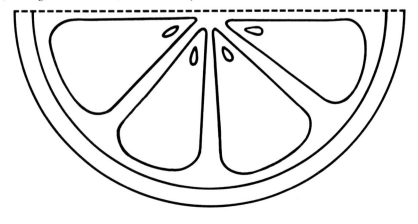

A "MOO-VING" GIFT

*O*ur *yummy Malted Milk Cookies are a natural for this handcrafted dairy cow bowl, which comes complete with a braided yarn tail and spool legs. Fresh from the kitchen, the milk chocolate-coated goodies are packed with the flavor of malted milk balls. This whimsical gift is sure to keep the conversation "moo-ving!"*

MALTED MILK COOKIES

- ⅔ cup margarine
- ½ cup sifted confectioners sugar
- 2¼ cups all-purpose flour
- ½ cup malted milk mix
- ¾ cup crushed malted milk ball candies
- 1 teaspoon vanilla extract
- 1 package (11.5 ounces) milk chocolate chips

In a mixing bowl, cream margarine and sugar. In a separate bowl, combine flour, malted milk mix, and crushed candies. Add to creamed mixture with vanilla and blend. (Mixture will be crumbly.) Knead dough with hands and shape into a smooth ball. Wrap in plastic wrap or aluminum foil; refrigerate 8 hours or overnight.

Preheat oven to 350 degrees. Shape dough into 1-inch balls and place on ungreased baking sheets; refrigerate 15 minutes. Bake 12 to 15 minutes or until lightly browned. Cool on wire racks.

To dip chocolate successfully, follow

Kitchen Tips, page 120, to melt and temper chocolate. Using a fondue fork, dip each cookie in melted chocolate. Place on wire rack with waxed paper underneath. Allow cookies to sit overnight to harden completely.

Yield: about 4 dozen cookies

COW BOWL

Note: Bowl is for decorative use and should only be used for dry foods. Wipe clean with a damp cloth.

You will need a single-serving wooden salad bowl, four wooden thread spools, black and cream acrylic paint, foam brush, flat paintbrush, black yarn, ⅜"w pink satin ribbon, matte

clear acrylic spray, hot glue gun, and glue sticks.

1. Paint bowl and spools with cream paint; allow to dry.
2. Use a pencil to draw spots on bowl; paint spots black. For hooves, paint one end of each spool black.
3. Apply two coats of acrylic spray to bowl and spools, allowing to dry between coats.
4. For tail, cut three equal lengths of yarn. Fold lengths in half; glue fold to one side of bowl near top edge. Braid tail; tie with a short piece of yarn to secure. Trim yarn 1" from tie and unravel ends. Tie ribbon in a bow around yarn tie; trim ends of ribbon.
5. Glue spools to bottom of bowl.

HAPPY HOUR SNACKS

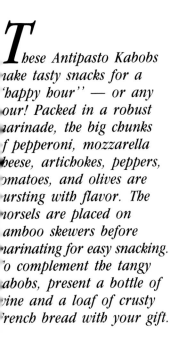

These Antipasto Kabobs make tasty snacks for a "happy hour" — or any hour! Packed in a robust marinade, the big chunks of pepperoni, mozzarella cheese, artichokes, peppers, tomatoes, and olives are bursting with flavor. The morsels are placed on bamboo skewers before marinating for easy snacking. To complement the tangy kabobs, present a bottle of wine and a loaf of crusty French bread with your gift.

ANTIPASTO KABOBS

MARINADE

½ cups olive oil
½ cups vinegar
2 tablespoons instant minced onion
2 teaspoons Italian seasoning
2 teaspoons garlic salt
2 teaspoons onion salt
½ teaspoons granulated sugar
1 teaspoon seasoned salt
1 teaspoon ground black pepper

KABOBS

8 ounces mozzarella cheese, cut
    into ½-inch cubes
1 can (14½ ounces) artichoke
    quarters
1 green pepper, cut into ½-inch
    squares
4 ounces pepperoni, cut into
    ½-inch slices
1 pint cherry tomatoes, halved
½ cup whole pitted black olives

For marinade, combine all ingredients in a jar, shaking to mix. For kabobs, trim bamboo skewers to fit in desired gift jar. Alternate kabob ingredients on skewers. Place kabobs in a 13 x 9 x 2-inch glass baking dish and pour marinade over. Cover and refrigerate 8 hours or overnight. To present, place kabobs in jar and add marinade to cover. Store covered in refrigerator.

Yield: about 16 kabobs

For waxed jar topper, cut a circle of cotton fabric 2¼" larger on all sides than jar lid. Use tongs to dip fabric into melted paraffin; allow excess paraffin to drip off. Working quickly, center fabric over lid and smooth down. Dip string into paraffin and tie into a bow around fabric and lid.

95

*C*reate a trio of hearty breads from a single recipe! Flavored with dry soup mixes, our Tomato-Basil, Herb, and Onion Breads are delicious served warm or toasted with a bowl of soup. For a variety of pleasing presentations, give a loaf on a woodburned cutting board, with a scalloped bread cloth, or in a colorful mesh bag with a set of soup bowls. Since the recipe makes six mini loaves — two of each flavor — you'll have plenty for giving.

'SOUP-ER' BREADS

    4 cups all-purpose flour
    2 teaspoons baking powder
    2 teaspoons baking soda
   ¼   cup dry tomato soup mix
   ¼   teaspoon basil
   ⅓   cup dry herb soup mix
    2 tablespoons dry golden onion
         soup mix
    2 eggs
   ½   cup butter or margarine
   ½   cup granulated sugar
    2 cups sour cream
   ⅔   cup milk

Preheat oven to 350 degrees. In a large bowl, combine flour, baking powder, and baking soda. Using 3 smaller bowls, place 1 ⅓ cups dry mixture into each bowl. Add tomato soup mix and basil to first bowl for

Tomato-Basil Bread, herb soup mix to second for Herb Bread, and onion soup mix to third for Onion Bread. Blend each thoroughly.

In a separate bowl, beat eggs, butter, and sugar until smooth. Stir in sour cream and milk. Pour 1 ⅓ cups batter into each dry mixture. Stir just until combined.

For a total of 6 loaves, spoon each batter into 2 greased and floured 5 ¾ x 3 x 2-inch loaf pans. Bake 30 to 35 minutes, testing for doneness with a toothpick. Cool in pans 10 minutes; remove and serve warm.

To reheat bread, wrap in aluminum foil and heat 10 to 15 minutes at 350 degrees or lightly toast in toaster oven.

Yield: 6 small loaves

Note: If desired, 1 or 2 varieties of soup may be used to flavor the entire batter mix. Adjust amount of dry soup mixture accordingly.

CUTTING BOARD

You will need a wooden cutting board with handle, tracing paper, graphite transfer paper, and woodburning pen.

1. Trace hearts pattern onto tracing paper. Use transfer paper to transfer pattern to cutting board.
2. Following manufacturer's instructions, use woodburning pen to burn design into cutting board.

BREAD CLOTH

You will need two 15″ squares of fabric, thread to match fabric, tracing paper, and removable fabric marking pen.

1. For pattern, fold tracing paper in half from top to bottom and again from left to right. Placing folds of paper along dashed lines of large heart pattern, trace pattern onto tracing paper and cut out. Unfold pattern.
2. Use pattern and follow Sewing Shapes, page 122, to make bread cloth from fabric squares. Press bread cloth and sew final closure by hand.

BREAKFAST IN BED

A breakfast-in-bed tray is a lovely way to pamper someone special. Sponge-painted roses lend an air of femininity to this simple rattan tray, making a pretty presentation for your surprise. Served with fresh croissants or pastries, Raspberry Fruit Spread is perfect for a light morning meal that pleases the eye as well as the palate.

RASPBERRY FRUIT SPREAD

- 2 packages (12 ounces each) frozen raspberries, thawed
- 1 envelope unflavored gelatin
- ¼ cup water
- ⅓ cup granulated sugar
- 1 tablespoon lemon juice

Drain raspberries, reserving ¼ cup juice. In a small cup, soften gelatin in water. Set aside.

In a medium saucepan, combine raspberries, reserved juice, sugar, and lemon juice. Bring to a boil. Reduce heat and simmer 5 minutes. Remove from heat and stir in gelatin mixture, blending well. Cool completely. Spoon into jars and refrigerate at least 8 hours before serving.

Yield: about 2 cups of spread

ROSE TRAY

You will need one rattan lap tray; tracing paper; craft knife; permanent felt-tip pen with fine point; two approx. 3 ½ " x 4 ½ " x ¾ " cellulose sponges; small, sharp scissors; pink, burgundy, and green acrylic paint; foam brushes; matte clear acrylic spray; and matte water-based varnish.

1. Wet sponges and allow to dry until stiff.
2. Trace rose and leaf patterns onto tracing paper. Cut shaded areas of patterns from tracing paper. Discard cutout pieces.
3. For rose sponge, position rose pattern on one sponge and use pen to draw inside cutout areas. Using craft knife, cut along pen lines approximately ⅜ " into sponge. Leaving outlined areas (shaded on pattern) raised ⅜ " for stamping, remove excess sponge around rose. Repeat with leaf pattern to make leaf sponge.
4. Dampen rose and leaf sponges and squeeze out excess water.
5. Reapplying paint as needed, use foam brush to apply an even coat of pink paint to rose sponge; stamp desired number of pink roses. Repeat with burgundy paint to stamp burgundy roses; repeat with green paint and leaf sponge to stamp leaves.
6. Spray tray with acrylic spray; allow to dry.
7. Apply two coats of varnish to tray, allowing to dry between coats.

PRETTY CREAMY COMBO

*L*ight and creamy, this Pistachio-Coconut Mousse Mix has an irresistible topping of crunchy nuts and toasted coconut. We packaged the mix in a pretty floral bag and dressed up a jar to hold the topping. To deliver the sweet gift, tuck the combo in a basket along with the super simple instructions for making the dessert. Later, the basket, bag, and jar can be used to hold soaps or potpourri.

PISTACHIO-COCONUT MOUSSE MIX

MOUSSE MIX

- 1 box (3½ ounces) instant coconut cream pudding mix
- 1 box (3½ ounces) instant pistachio pudding mix
- 2 envelopes (one 2.6-ounce box) whipped topping mix

TOPPING

- ⅔ cup flaked coconut, toasted
- ⅓ cup chopped pistachio nuts

For mousse mix, combine all ingredients in a large bowl. Place mixture in airtight container or resealable plastic bag. For topping, combine coconut and nuts; place in a small jar.

Yield: about 2 cups of mix and 1 cup of topping

To serve: Combine 1 cup mix with 1¼ cups milk in a large bowl. Beat with an electric mixer at high speed until fluffy, about 3 to 4 minutes. Serve immediately or store covered in refrigerator up to 2 hours. Sprinkle with topping before serving.

Yield: about 4 servings

FABRIC BAG AND JAR

You will need a jar and lid with screw ring, one 5½" x 24" piece of fabric, 1 yd of ⅛" dia. twisted satin cord, acrylic paint to match fabric, foam brush, thread to match fabric, one 5" square of craft batting, matte clear acrylic spray, and craft glue.

1. For bag, cut a 5½" x 18" piece from fabric and follow Steps 2 - 4 of Fabric Bag instructions, page 122.

2. For jar, paint screw ring; allow to dry. Spray ring with acrylic spray; allow to dry. Using flat piece of lid as a pattern, cut a circle from batting and remaining fabric. Glue batting to flat piece of lid. Glue fabric to batting along edge. Glue lid inside ring.

3. (Note: To prevent cord from untwisting, apply glue to end of cord and to area to be cut. Allow glue to dry before cutting.) Measure around screw ring; cut cord to fit and glue cord around ring. Cut a 22" length of cord for bag.

4. Place a plastic bag of mix in fabric bag; tie cord into a bow around bag.

COUNTRY GIFT BAGS

*I*t's easy to add a homespun touch to any gift! With our creative techniques, you can transform ordinary paper sacks into cute country gift bags. Crafty closings, fabric scraps, buttons, and other odds and ends give each one a charm all its own. To fill your bags, use any of the cookies, candies, or snacks in this book — or add purchased goodies for quick gifts. Small bags are just right for individual portions, and larger ones can be used for family-size gifts.

COUNTRY-STYLE BAGS

COUNTRY TRIMMINGS

Soft country fabrics and sweet motifs provide endless decorating combinations that will turn a plain brown paper bag into a charming gift bag!

You may need tracing paper, craft knife, graphite transfer paper, cardboard, fabric scraps, pinking shears, felt-tip pen with fine point, fabric glue, embroidery floss, buttons, and a large needle.

● For patchwork quilt bag, trace quilt block pattern onto tracing paper. Use transfer paper to transfer design to one side of bag. Place cardboard inside bag behind design; use craft knife to cut out design. Glue a piece of fabric inside bag behind cutout. Trace square and small heart patterns onto tracing paper and cut out. Use patterns and cut heart and square from fabric; glue shapes to outside of bag.

● For fabric shapes, trace pattern onto tracing paper and cut out. Use pattern and cut shape from fabric; glue shape to bag. Use a combination of different shapes to give your bag additional charm.

● A square of contrasting fabric pinked along the edges and placed behind another cutout fabric shape will make the shape stand out more.

● Make a patriotic heart of blue and red fabrics sporting stars and stripes. Cut a heart from striped fabric; cut the top half of another heart from blue fabric. After fringing blue fabric along the straight edge, glue the heart pieces to your bag.

● For homespun appeal, "sew" it all together using a button and floss or add "stitching" around fabric shapes with a felt-tip pen.

COUNTRY TOPPINGS

A little creativity will top off your bag with a homespun finish.

● Trim the top of the bag straight for a neat and tidy finish.

● Cut curves along the top for a scalloped edge.

● Give your bag a "picket fence" look by cutting points along the top.

● Leave the top as it is for a natural look.

COUNTRY TOUCHES

Your gift isn't complete until you fill the bag and close it. Give it your own country touch by adding coordinating fabric squares for filler or by closing the bag with a crafty finish.

You may need fabric scraps, pinking shears, hole punch, ribbon, cotton cord, buttons, jute, beads, and a large needle.

● After placing a food gift in the bag, give your gift a homespun touch by adding a fringed piece of fabric to fill up the bag.

● Tie a couple of strands of narrow ribbon around the top of the bag, then thread them through a button and tie into a bow. Knot ends of streamers to complete the closure.

● For a primitive finish, thread a large needle with jute and "sew" around the top of the bag. Tie jute into a bow and knot wooden beads on streamers.

● For a secure closure, fold top of bag down and punch holes near folded edge. Thread ribbon or a pinked fabric strip through holes and tie into a bow.

● Fold top of bag down and use large needle to thread cotton cord through folded area. Tie cord into a bow and knot ends of streamers.

● For decorative appeal, fanfold top of bag at ½" intervals. Use large needle to thread ribbon through top fold near each side of bag; pull sides up to meet and tie ribbon into a bow.

EMERGENCY LUNCH KIT

In case of emergency, here's a quick, hot lunch! Perfect for someone starting a new job, this little lunch kit will come in handy when bad weather or a hectic schedule makes going out inconvenient. Simply adding hot water to the instant Potato Soup Mix makes a thick, creamy cup of soup. To complete the kit, add some cheesy Parmesan-Herb Nibbles and include a colorful mug, spoon, and napkin.

POTATO SOUP MIX

1 ¾   cups instant mashed potatoes
1 ½   cups nonfat dry milk
  2   tablespoons instant chicken
       bouillon
  2   teaspoons dried minced onion
1 ½   teaspoons seasoned salt
  1   teaspoon dried parsley
 ¼   teaspoon dried whole thyme
 ¼   teaspoon ground white pepper
 ⅛   teaspoon turmeric

Combine all ingredients in a large bowl, mixing until completely blended. Store in airtight container.

Yield: about 2 ½ cups of mix

To serve: Place ¼ cup soup mix in a soup bowl or mug. Add 1 cup boiling water and stir until smooth. Let soup sit 1 to 2 minutes to thicken slightly.

PARMESAN-HERB NIBBLES

 1   cup all-purpose flour
 ½   teaspoon baking powder
 ¼   teaspoon salt
 ⅛   teaspoon cayenne pepper
 1   teaspoon Fines Herbes
     (in grocery spice section)
 ⅓   cup butter or margarine
 ⅔   cup grated Parmesan cheese
 3   egg yolks
 2   teaspoons water

Preheat oven to 400 degrees. In a large bowl, sift together first 4 ingredients. Stir in herbs. With a pastry blender or 2 knives, cut in butter and cheese until mixture resembles a coarse meal. Stir in egg yolks and water. Place dough on a lightly floured surface and knead until smooth, about 2 minutes. Roll out dough to ⅛-inch thickness. With a paring knife, cut dough vertically into 1-inch wide strips; cut 1-inch wide strips horizontally to make small squares. Carefully lift squares from surface with flat side of knife and place on greased baking sheets. Bake 8 to 10 minutes or until lightly browned. Cool completely before storing in airtight container.

Yield: about 6 dozen squares

EMERGENCY LUNCH KIT

You will need a box (we used a 10 ½ " x 5 ½ " x 3 ¾ " shoe box), 3"w bandaging gauze, wrapping paper, tracing paper, white poster board, red and blue felt-tip markers, hole punch, transparent tape, and spray adhesive.

1. To cover box, follow Gift Box 1 instructions, page 123.
2. Trace cross pattern onto tracing paper and cut out. Use pattern and cut desired number of crosses from poster board.
3. Apply spray adhesive to wrong sides of crosses. Place crosses in desired positions on box and food containers; press firmly to secure.
4. Trace tag pattern onto tracing paper and cut out. Use pattern and cut tag from poster board. Use markers to write "Emergency! OPEN ONLY IN CASE OF LUNCH" on tag. Punch hole in tag near pointed end.
5. Fold gauze in half lengthwise. Thread tag onto gauze and tie gauze into a bow around box.

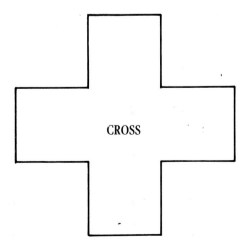

CROSS

TAG

A HONEY OF A GIFT

*Y*our friends will be abuzz with pleasure when they taste our Honey-Almond Popcorn! A combination of fluffy popcorn, crunchy almonds, and golden honey, it's a sweet treat that's fun to eat. To present it, paint a basket with bees and our cute verse. Chenille bees make "bee-utiful" accents.

HONEY-ALMOND POPCORN

½ cup unpopped popcorn
¾ cup honey
½ cup granulated sugar
½ cup butter or margarine
½ cup light corn syrup
2 cups whole almonds
½ teaspoon baking soda
¼ teaspoon salt

Pop popcorn following package instructions. In a large saucepan, bring honey, sugar, butter, and corn syrup to a boil, stirring constantly. Reduce heat to medium-low and simmer 5 minutes, stirring occasionally. Remove from heat and stir in almonds, baking soda, and salt.

Preheat oven to 250 degrees. Spread popped popcorn on a greased 15 x 10 x 1-inch jellyroll pan. Pour honey mixture over, stirring to combine. Bake 1 hour, stirring every 15 minutes. Remove from oven and immediately turn onto waxed paper to cool. Break into pieces and store in airtight container.

Yield: about 4 quarts of popcorn

BEE BASKET

You will need a market basket, water-based wood stain, foam brush, matte clear acrylic spray, a soft cloth, yellow and black paint markers with fine points, graphite transfer paper, and tracing paper.

1. Apply one coat of stain to basket and remove excess with soft cloth; allow to dry.
2. Apply three coats of acrylic spray to basket, allowing to dry between coats.
3. Trace bee pattern onto tracing paper. Use transfer paper to transfer bees onto basket.
4. Use a pencil to draw dots and write "What does the Bee do? Brings home the honey" on basket.
5. Use paint markers to paint bees and to paint over dots and words; allow to dry.
6. Apply one coat of acrylic spray to basket; allow to dry.

A FLAVORFUL SURPRISE

Lightly spiced with cinnamon, this Orange Sugar is a flavorful surprise. It's great for sprinkling on hot cereal and fresh fruit or as a substitute for ordinary sugar in baking. For giving, pour the sugar into a bow-tied jar and attach the recipe for our tasty Orange Muffins, one of many ways to enjoy the special sugar. You may even want to present a fresh batch of muffins for sampling.

ORANGE SUGAR

 ⅔ cup grated orange peel
       (about 7 large oranges)
 4 cups granulated sugar
1½ teaspoons ground cinnamon

Place all ingredients in a blender or food processor fitted with a steel blade. Process until ingredients are completely mixed. Sprinkle over hot cereals or fresh fruit, or substitute for granulated sugar in baking. Store in airtight container in refrigerator.

Yield: about 4 cups of sugar

ORANGE MUFFINS

 ½ cup shortening
1¼ cups Orange Sugar, divided
 2 eggs
 2 cups all-purpose flour
 1 teaspoon baking soda
 1 cup buttermilk
 ½ cup golden raisins
 ⅓ cup orange juice

Preheat oven to 350 degrees. In a large bowl, cream shortening and 1 cup Orange Sugar until smooth. Add eggs, beating until fluffy. In a separate bowl, sift together flour and baking soda. Add to creamed mixture along with buttermilk, beating until blended. Stir in raisins. Fill greased and floured muffin pans two-thirds full with batter. Bake 15 to 18 minutes, testing for doneness with a toothpick. While muffins are still warm, brush with orange juice and sprinkle with ¼ cup Orange Sugar. Store in airtight container.

Yield: about 1½ dozen muffins

*D*elight someone who loves the "purr-fect" combination of cookies and milk with these Triple Peanut Butter Cookies! Topped with chunky peanuts, they feature a layer of creamy peanut butter sandwiched between two rich peanut butter cookies. A handcrafted kitty makes an entertaining keepsake to top off your gift basket.

TRIPLE PEANUT BUTTER COOKIES

- ½ cup granulated sugar
- ½ cup brown sugar, firmly packed
- ½ cup shortening
- ¾ cup smooth peanut butter, divided
- 2 tablespoons light corn syrup
- 1 tablespoon milk
- ½ teaspoon vanilla extract
- 1½ cups all-purpose flour
- ½ teaspoon baking soda
- ¼ teaspoon salt
- ½ cup chopped roasted peanuts

In a large bowl, cream sugars, shortening, and ½ cup peanut butter. Blend in corn syrup, milk, and vanilla. In a separate bowl, sift together next 3 ingredients. Add to creamed mixture, mixing well. Shape dough into a 1½-inch dia. roll. Wrap in plastic wrap and chill at least 2 hours.

Preheat oven to 350 degrees. Slice dough into ⅛-inch thick slices. Place half of the slices on ungreased baking sheets and spread each with ½ teaspoon peanut butter. Top with remaining slices; seal edges with a fork. Sprinkle peanuts over tops of cookies, gently pressing nuts into the dough. Bake 12 to 15 minutes or until lightly browned. Cool on wire racks. Store in airtight container.

Yield: about 2½ dozen cookies

CAT BASKET

You will need a basket with handle, one 12″ x 20″ piece of unbleached muslin, instant coffee, cellulose sponge, thread to match muslin, tracing paper, fabric marking pencil, small crochet hook (to turn fabric), polyester fiberfill, black permanent felt-tip pen with fine point, pink colored pencil, large needle, jute, hot glue gun, and glue sticks.

1. Trace body, arm, and leg patterns onto tracing paper and cut out. For each shape, cut two pieces of muslin 1″ larger than pattern on all sides. Follow Sewing Shapes, page 122, to make one body, two arms, and two legs.
2. For ears, use Running Stitch, page 124, and stitch where indicated by dashed lines on pattern.
3. Stuff shapes with fiberfill; sew final closures of all shapes by hand.
4. Use pen to draw face; use pink pencil to blush cheeks.
5. For each arm, thread needle with a length of jute. Insert needle through arm, then body, at one ●; do not pull jute all the way through. Insert needle back through body, then arm, at same ●. Knot ends of jute together and trim ends. Repeat to attach legs at ◆'s.

6. Dissolve 1 tablespoon instant coffee in 1 cup hot water. Use sponge to apply coffee to cat; allow to dry.
7. Glue bottom of cat to basket.

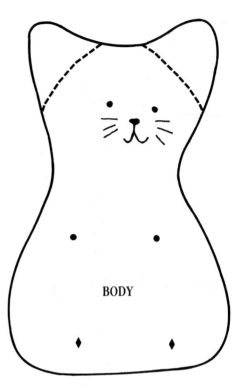

BODY

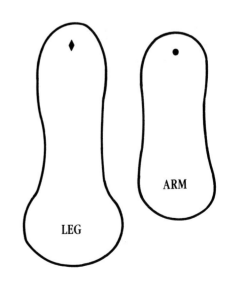

LEG

ARM

CUPBOARD COOKIES

*C*hock-full of good
things from your pantry,
a jar of these crispy
Cupboard Cookies is a nice
way to send warm wishes.
When the jar is refilled,
the reversible tag will let
snackers know whether the
goodies are homemade or
store-bought.

CUPBOARD COOKIES

    1 cup butter or margarine, softened
    1 cup granulated sugar
    1 cup brown sugar, firmly packed
    1 egg
    1 cup vegetable oil
    1 teaspoon vanilla extract
    1 cup old-fashioned rolled oats
    1 cup crushed cornflake cereal
    ½ cup flaked coconut
    ½ cup chopped pecans
    ½ cup miniature semisweet
       chocolate chips
 3 ½ cups all-purpose flour
    1 teaspoon baking soda
    1 teaspoon salt
       Granulated sugar

Preheat oven to 325 degrees. In a
large bowl, cream butter and sugars
until light and fluffy. Add egg, oil,
and vanilla, beating well. Stir in next
5 ingredients. Sift flour, baking soda,
and salt into mixture; mix thoroughly.
Shape dough into 1 ½ -inch balls. Roll
in granulated sugar and place on
ungreased baking sheets. Flatten with
a fork dipped in cold water. Bake
10 to 12 minutes or until lightly
browned around edges. Cool cookies
on baking sheets before removing.
Store in airtight container.

Yield: about 8 dozen cookies

For reversible mini pillow tag, stitch
designs on Rustico (14 ct) using
2 strands of floss for Cross Stitch.
Follow Mini Pillow instructions,
page 122, to complete tag.

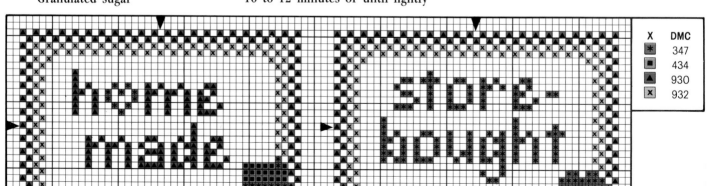

X	DMC
✳	347
■	434
▲	930
✕	932

WESTERN SURPRISE

Moist and spicy, this sweet bread has a secret ingredient that will keep your friends guessing. They'll never believe that it's made with a can of pork and beans! For a presentation that's packed with the spirit of the Old West, bake the bread in tin cans and accent them with bright bandanas.

PORK 'N' BEAN BREAD

- 2 cups granulated sugar
- 1 cup vegetable oil
- 3 eggs
- 1 can (16 ounces) pork and beans, drained
- 2 cups all-purpose flour
- 1 teaspoon ground cinnamon
- ½ teaspoon baking powder
- ½ teaspoon baking soda
- 1 cup raisins
- 1 teaspoon vanilla extract

Preheat oven to 325 degrees. In a large bowl, mix sugar, oil, eggs, and beans, beating until smooth. In a separate bowl, combine next 4 ingredients. Add to bean mixture, stirring just until combined. Stir in raisins and vanilla. Fill 5 greased and floured 16-ounce cans two-thirds full with batter.* Place cans on a baking sheet and bake 45 to 50 minutes, testing for doneness with a toothpick. Cool completely on a wire rack before removing bread from cans.

Bread may also be baked in two 8½ x 4½ x 2¾-inch loaf pans at 325 degrees for 50 to 55 minutes.

Yield: 5 cans or 2 loaves of bread

*Note: If desired, open each can, leaving lid attached at 1 small point. Bend each lid away from can opening to allow bread to rise while baking.

For bandana, we cut a 14½″ square from a standard bandana and hemmed the cut edges. It was folded in half diagonally, rolled up, and tied around a can of Pork 'N' Bean Bread.

Loaded with all the makin's for a Tex-Mex meal, this Southwest basket is a portable fiesta! Our wonderful Three-Bean Chili combines a variety of beans with chunks of pepper, onion, and tomato. Cheese, crackers, and hot sauce complete the hearty meal. The festive basket, lined with a bright Southwestern print cloth, is simply decorated with burlap and raffia. A star crafted with dried beans and peppers adds an impressive finish.

THREE-BEAN CHILI

2 pounds ground round
1 tablespoon vegetable oil
1 large red onion, cut into chunks
1 large green pepper, cut into chunks
1 jalapeño pepper, seeded and diced
2 cloves garlic, minced
1 cup red wine
½ cup Worcestershire sauce
2 tablespoons chili powder
1 teaspoon dry mustard
1 teaspoon celery seeds
1 teaspoon salt
½ teaspoon ground black pepper
3 cans (14.5 ounces each) Italian-style tomatoes, chopped with liquid
1 can (15 ounces) black beans
1 can (15 ounces) garbanzo beans
1 can (15 ounces) kidney beans

Brown meat in a large Dutch oven; drain and remove from pan. Add oil to Dutch oven and sauté onion, green pepper, jalapeño, and garlic until soft, about 6 minutes. Add wine and Worcestershire; simmer 10 minutes. Stir in next 5 ingredients and simmer 10 minutes longer. Add tomatoes, beans (undrained), and meat to Dutch oven. Heat chili to boiling; reduce heat, cover, and simmer 30 minutes, stirring occasionally. Remove cover and simmer 30 minutes longer.

Yield: about 4½ quarts of chili

SOUTHWEST BASKET

You will need a basket with handle; burlap (amount determined by size of basket); natural-colored raffia; mat board or heavy cardboard; tracing paper; black acrylic paint; flat paintbrush; five small dried red chili peppers; dried kidney beans, black beans, and garbanzo beans; hot glue gun; glue sticks; glossy clear acrylic spray; and craft glue.

1. For side of basket, measure circumference of basket just below rim and add 1″. Cut a 2½″ wide strip of burlap the determined length. Fold strip in half lengthwise and hot glue below basket rim, overlapping ends.
2. To cover basket handle, measure length of handle and multiply by 2½. Cut a 2″ wide strip of burlap the determined length, piecing as needed.
3. Overlapping long edges, tightly wrap burlap strip around handle; hot glue at ends of handle to secure.
4. Wrap handle with one strand of raffia; hot glue ends of raffia to secure. Repeat with a second strand, wrapping in opposite direction and crisscrossing first strand.
5. For star, trace pattern onto tracing paper and cut out. Use pattern and cut one star from mat board.
6. Paint star black; allow to dry.
7. (Note: Use craft glue to assemble star.) With stems of peppers at center of star, glue peppers to star. Glue one kidney bean between each pair of peppers. Glue one garbanzo bean to each kidney bean close to center of star. Glue black beans to cover remaining part of star. Spray star with acrylic spray and allow to dry.
8. Tie several strands of raffia into a bow; hot glue star to center of bow. Hot glue bow to basket handle.

HAPPY BAGS

A rainbow of colors and an assortment of peek-a-boo cutouts lined with cellophane or tissue paper make these gift bags a bright delight! To send greetings for any occasion, use ribbons, stickers, and handwritten messages to personalize each sack. Fill your happy bags with goodies from this book or purchased treats.

HAPPY BAGS

DRESSING IT UP
Let your imagination run wild! Use your creativity and the ideas shown here to turn a plain brown paper bag into a gift bag dressed up for a very special occasion.

You may need tracing paper, craft knife, cardboard, graphite transfer paper, colored cellophane, colored felt-tip pens, stickers, gummed stars, ribbon, craft glue, and transparent tape.

● For cutouts, trace desired pattern onto tracing paper. Use transfer paper to transfer pattern to one side of bag. Place cardboard inside bag behind design; use craft knife to cut out design.

● Taping colored cellophane behind your cutout designs adds a bright touch. You may wish to use small pieces of different colors of cellophane. Or you can use a large piece of cellophane and make the whole design one color.

● Write a personal message on your bag with felt-tip pens. Pens can also be used to add details such as balloon strings, holly berries, or decorative outlines around the cutouts.

● Add nifty accents by affixing gummed stars, stickers, or ribbon bows to your bag.

● For a quick and easy decoration, incorporate a purchased sticker into a personal saying that shows just how you feel.

TOPPING IT OFF
Don't stop with the front of your bag! A little embellishment at the top ensures that your bag is one of a kind.

You may need scissors, pinking shears, and a hole punch.

● Cutting the top edge straight is a simple way to give your bag a neat and tidy appearance.

● Give your bag a lacy effect by scalloping the top edge and punching holes in the centers of the scallops.

● Trim the top edge of the bag straight; then give it ''fringe'' by cutting into the edge at close intervals.

● Give your bag a different look by using pinking shears to cut the top edge.

● For a delicate touch, cut the top edge of the bag to a point, then cut scallops along the sloped edges.

● Don't overlook the obvious! The tops of some bags look great just the way they are.

FILLING IT UP
Your food gift may not fill the entire bag. That means there's still room to have some fun!

You may need colored cellophane; plain, printed, and colored tissue paper; and shredded cellophane gift bag filler.

● If your cutouts are not backed with cellophane, line the bag with tissue paper so no one will be able to peek at what's inside!

● After placing your food gift in the bag, finish filling it up with one or more sheets of loosely bunched tissue paper or cellophane. Combining sheets of tissue paper and cellophane adds extra pizzazz.

● Shredded cellophane filler stuffed here and there provides sparkly appeal.

CLOSING REMARKS
Close your bag securely, tie it loosely at the top, or leave it completely open. The type of closure you choose will give your bag a character all its own.

You may need a hole punch, large needle, ribbon, cotton cord, beads, bells, and braided jute.

● Use strands of narrow ribbon to tie a cheerful bow around the top of the bag. Knot bow streamers near the ends for a fancy touch.

● Thread needle with festive ribbon and ''sew'' ribbon around the top of the bag. Add a bell or other small trinket and tie ribbon into a bow.

● For a more secure closure, fold the top of the bag down and punch holes near the folded edge. Thread jute through holes and tie into a bow.

● For a quick closure, fold the top of the bag down and use large needle to thread cord through folded area of bag; tie cord into a bow. Knot beads near ends of streamers for a splash of color.

LITTLE LEMON BASKETS

Let Mother Nature help with the packaging on this unique gift! These attractive lemon baskets are perfect for holding our Lemony Cranberry Juice Mulls. Packed with brown sugar, lemon peel, and spices, the mulls make a wonderful hot drink when added to cranberry juice. Whether you give several in a colorful gift bag or use them as party favors, your good taste will be appreciated sip after sip.

LEMONY CRANBERRY JUICE MULLS

⅓ cup brown sugar, firmly packed
4 (3 to 4-inch) cinnamon sticks, broken into pieces
3 teaspoons whole allspice
2 whole nutmegs, crushed
3 teaspoons grated lemon peel
4 large lemons

For mull mixture, combine all ingredients except lemons in a small bowl. To make each lemon basket, refer to Fig. 1 and vertically cut a ¼-inch wide strip at center of lemon for the handle, cutting through only half of the lemon. Cut horizontally from each tip of the lemon to the handle. Remove wedges from both sides; scoop out pulp.

Fig. 1

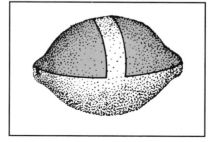

For mulls, divide mull mixture into fourths and spoon onto four 2-inch squares of cheesecloth; wrap cheesecloth around mixture and tie with string. Place spice bundles in lemon baskets. Wrap mulls in plastic wrap; tie with ribbon. Store in refrigerator.

Yield: 4 mulls

To make mulled cranberry juice: Place 1 mull and 1½ quarts cranberry juice in a large saucepan. Bring to a boil; simmer 15 minutes.

PESTO NOW, PESTO LATER

This robust Pesto will be a big hit with herb lovers or gourmet cooks — or anyone who loves good food! A blend of fresh basil, garlic, pine nuts, and Parmesan cheese, the Italian sauce is delicious tossed with pasta, spread on meats or bread, or stirred into sour cream for a vegetable dip. A basket stenciled with basil leaves is perfect for presenting the gift. And when you include a basil plant with the sauce, your friend can enjoy pesto now and pesto later!

PESTO

    2 cups fresh basil leaves,
         firmly packed
    3 cloves garlic, minced
    ½ cup pine nuts
    ½ cup chopped fresh parsley
    ¾ cup grated Parmesan cheese
    1 teaspoon salt
    ½ teaspoon ground black pepper
    ⅔ cup olive oil

Place all ingredients except oil in a blender or food processor fitted with a steel blade. Process until ingredients are finely chopped. With processor running, pour oil into mixture. Store in airtight container in refrigerator.

Yield: about 2 cups of pesto

Serving Suggestions: Toss with cooked pasta; spread on meat and broil; spread on bread and bake; or add to sour cream for a vegetable dip.

BASIL BASKET

You will need a basket with area suitable for stenciling; matte ivory spray paint; grey, rust, and green acrylic paint; foam brushes; soft cloths; tagboard (manila folder); tracing paper; graphite transfer paper; craft knife; small stencil brush; paper towels; matte clear acrylic spray; and a tongue depressor and brown felt-tip pen with fine point (for plant poke).

1. Spray paint basket; allow to dry.
2. Mix 2 parts grey paint to 1 part water. Paint basket with diluted paint and remove excess with soft cloth. Allow to dry.
3. Painting crevices and raised areas only, repeat Step 2 using rust paint.

4. Use green paint and follow How To Stencil, page 122, to stencil leaves on basket; allow to dry.
5. For plant poke, spray paint tongue depressor; allow to dry. Use brown pen to write ''BASIL'' on tongue depressor.
6. Spray basket and plant poke with acrylic spray; allow to dry.

NUT SAMPLER

Packed with a bountiful harvest of nuts, this sampler features three delicious varieties. Peppy Pecans are spiced with chili powder and cayenne pepper, and Barbecued Peanuts are easy to make with purchased sauce. A coffee-flavored praline coating gives Mocha Walnuts an unforgettable flavor. We decorated our tin with a false-grained finish and divided it to hold all three choices, but you may want to give only one or two.

BARBECUED PEANUTS

    3 cups unsalted dry-roasted
         peanuts
 ⅓ cup mesquite smoke-flavored
         barbecue sauce
 ½ teaspoon onion salt

Preheat oven to 300 degrees. In a large bowl, combine all ingredients. Spread nuts on a lightly greased baking sheet and bake 20 minutes, stirring after 10 minutes. Cool completely and store in an airtight container.

Yield: about 3 cups of nuts

PEPPY PECANS

 ⅓ cup butter or margarine
    2 tablespoons Worcestershire sauce
 1 ½ teaspoons garlic salt
 ½ teaspoon seasoned salt
 ½ teaspoon ground cumin
 ½ teaspoon chili powder
 ⅛ teaspoon cayenne pepper
    3 cups pecan halves
    2 tablespoons coarse salt

Preheat oven to 325 degrees. In a large saucepan, melt butter over medium-low heat. Add next 6 ingredients; simmer 5 minutes. Add nuts, stirring to coat. Spread nuts on a baking sheet and bake 15 to 20 minutes, stirring after 10 minutes. Remove from oven and sprinkle with coarse salt; cool completely. Store in an airtight container.

Yield: about 3 cups of nuts

MOCHA WALNUTS

 ½ cup granulated sugar
 ½ cup brown sugar, firmly packed
 ½ cup sour cream
    1 tablespoon instant coffee granules
 ½ teaspoon ground cinnamon
 ¼ teaspoon ground nutmeg
    1 teaspoon vanilla extract
    3 cups walnut halves

In a large saucepan, combine first 6 ingredients, mixing well. Cook over medium heat, stirring constantly, to soft ball stage (238 degrees). Remove from heat and stir in vanilla. Add nuts, stirring to coat. Spread nuts on a buttered baking sheet. Cool completely and break into pieces. Store in an airtight container.

Yield: about 4 ½ cups of nuts

FALSE-GRAINED TIN

You will need a tin (we used an 8″ dia. tin); the following Folk Art® products: Apple Butter Brown Antiquing, Thickener, Harvest Gold acrylic paint, and Waterbase Varnish; gesso; foam brushes; plastic wrap; paper towel; poster board; and craft glue.

1. Apply 2 coats of gesso, then 2 coats of Harvest Gold paint to tin and lid, allowing to dry between coats.
2. For glaze, mix 1 tablespoon Antiquing and 2 tablespoons Thickener in a small bowl.
3. For lid, apply 1 coat of glaze to lid. Working quickly and wiping excess glaze from finger on a paper towel, use pad of index finger to stamp fingerprints along edge on top of lid. For mottled effect, use a crumpled piece of plastic wrap to stamp center of lid; allow to dry.
4. For side of tin, repeat Step 3, stamping fingerprints along bottom edge of tin; use plastic wrap to stamp side of tin.
5. Apply 2 coats of varnish to tin and lid, allowing to dry between coats.
6. To determine height of divider pieces, measure height of tin and subtract ¼″. To determine length of divider pieces, measure diameter of tin. Cut 3 pieces of poster board the determined measurements. Match short ends and fold each piece of poster board in half. Refer to photo and glue pieces together at folds; allow to dry. Insert divider in tin, trimming to fit if necessary.

Treat a favorite couple to lunch for two! Filled with fresh summer vegetables, Spicy Gazpacho is served chilled for a refreshing light meal. Dilly Cheese Scones are a delicious accompaniment to the chunky soup. To add charm to your lunch basket, make a pair of pretty place mats; then roll and tie them with matching ribbon for an elegant touch.

DILLY CHEESE SCONES

2 cups all-purpose flour
1 tablespoon baking powder
2 teaspoons dried dill weed
1 teaspoon salt
½ teaspoon dry mustard
¼ cup butter or margarine
1 cup (4 ounces) grated sharp
    Cheddar cheese
1 cup milk
1 egg
1 teaspoon water

Preheat oven to 425 degrees. In a large bowl, combine first 5 ingredients. Cut in butter with a pastry blender or 2 knives until mixture resembles a coarse meal. Stir in cheese. Make a well in the center of mixture; pour in milk. Mix with a fork just until blended.

With floured hands, turn out dough onto a lightly floured surface and pat out to ½-inch thickness. Using a 2-inch round biscuit cutter, cut out scones and place on an ungreased baking sheet. In a small cup, blend egg and water; lightly brush over scones. Bake 12 to 15 minutes or until tops are golden brown. Serve warm.

Yield: about 1 dozen scones

Note: To reheat scones, wrap in aluminum foil and bake 10 minutes at 400 degrees.

SPICY GAZPACHO

3 tomatoes, chopped
1 cucumber, chopped
1 green pepper, chopped
1 onion, chopped
¾ cup chopped fresh parsley
2 cloves garlic, minced
3½ cups liquid Bloody Mary mix
¼ cup white wine vinegar
¼ cup olive oil
½ teaspoon salt
¼ teaspoon ground black pepper

In a large bowl, combine first 6 ingredients. In a separate bowl, use a wire whisk to blend remaining ingredients. Add liquid to vegetable mixture, stirring to combine. Cover and refrigerate at least 2 hours before serving. Serve cold. Store in airtight container in refrigerator.

Yield: about 8 cups of soup

PLACE MATS

For each place mat, you will need two 13½" x 19" pieces of fabric for place mat, two 11" x 16½" pieces of fabric for inset, and thread to match fabrics.

1. For place mat, place large fabric pieces right sides together. Leaving an opening for turning and using a ¼" seam allowance, sew fabric pieces together. Cut corners diagonally and turn right side out; press. Sew final closure by hand.
2. For inset, repeat Step 1 with remaining fabric pieces.
3. Center inset on place mat and pin in place. Sew pieces together close to edges of inset.

KITCHEN TIPS

To bake in glass ovenware: Reduce oven temperature by 25 degrees.

•

To beat egg whites: For greatest volume, beat egg whites at room temperature in a clean, dry bowl.

•

To blanch almonds: Place 1 cup water in a 1-quart bowl or casserole; cover. Microwave at High 3 minutes. Add 1 cup whole shelled almonds. Microwave at High 1 minute uncovered; drain and remove peel from nuts. Dry on paper towels.

•

To cut cookie shapes: Dip cookie or biscuit cutter in water to keep dough from sticking to cutter.

•

To decorate with melted candy: Place ½ cup candy melts or chopped almond bark in a pint-size, resealable plastic bag; do not seal. Microwave at Medium (50%) 2 to 3 minutes, turning bag after each minute. Candy should be soft to the touch and warm, not hot. Use scissors to cut a small tip from one lower corner of the bag. Seal bag; squeeze melted candy through corner of bag to decorate as desired.

•

To dip chocolate successfully: Temper chocolate by melting chopped or shaved chocolate in the top of a double boiler (or in a bowl over a saucepan of water) over hot, not boiling, water. Use a candy thermometer and heat chocolate to 110 to 120 degrees for *dark chocolate* or to 110 to 115 degrees for *white* or *milk chocolate*. Next, place the container of melted chocolate in a bowl of cold water. Cool chocolate to 85 degrees, stirring occasionally. Use chocolate for dipping as desired.

•

To dissolve dry yeast: Use warm water (110 to 115 degrees) when dissolving yeast. Higher temperatures kill yeast and prevent breads from rising properly.

•

To grate cheese easily: Place wrapped cheese in freezer for 10 to 20 minutes before grating.

•

To juice citrus fruit: Microwave whole fruit at High 20 to 30 seconds before cutting and squeezing to increase the amount of juice.

•

To measure honey or syrup: Lightly spray measuring cup or spoon with cooking spray before measuring. The liquid will release easily from the cup or spoon for more accurate measurement.

•

To peel and seed tomatoes: Immerse whole tomatoes in boiling water 1 minute; then immerse in cold water 1 minute. Drain and remove skin. For seeding, halve tomato vertically from stem end. Hold tomato in palm of hand and squeeze to remove seeds and juice. This will reduce watery results when cooking with tomatoes.

•

To ripen bananas: Place peeled, whole bananas on an ungreased baking sheet and bake 8 minutes at 350 degrees.

To seal jars for canning: Wash and dry jars, lids, and bands. Place jars on a rack in a large Dutch oven. Place lids in a saucepan; cover jars and lids with water. Bring both pans to a boil; boil 10 minutes. Drain and dry jars and lids completely before filling. Seal jars with lids and invert jars 5 minutes. Turn upright and cool before storing.

•

To soften butter or margarine: Remove wrapper from butter and place on a plate. Microwave 20 to 30 seconds at Medium-Low (30%) for 1 stick.

•

To soften cream cheese: Remove wrapper from cream cheese and place on a plate. Microwave 1 to 1½ minutes at Medium (50%) for one 8-ounce package or 30 to 45 seconds for one 3-ounce package.

•

To substitute dried herbs for fresh: Use ½ teaspoon dried herbs for 1 tablespoon fresh chopped herbs.

•

To toast coconut: Spread a thin layer of coconut on an ungreased baking sheet and bake 10 minutes at 350 degrees, stirring occasionally.

•

To toast nuts: Spread nuts evenly on an ungreased baking sheet and bake 10 to 15 minutes at 350 degrees, stirring occasionally.

EQUIVALENT MEASUREMENTS

1 tablespoon	=	3 teaspoons
⅛ cup or 1 fluid ounce	=	2 tablespoons
¼ cup	=	4 tablespoons
⅓ cup	=	5 ⅓ tablespoons
½ cup	=	8 tablespoons
¾ cup	=	12 tablespoons
1 cup	=	16 tablespoons
1 cup or ½ pint	=	8 fluid ounces
2 cups or 1 pint	=	16 fluid ounces
1 quart	=	2 pints
½ gallon	=	2 quarts
1 gallon	=	4 quarts

HELPFUL FOOD EQUIVALENTS

½ cup butter	=	1 stick butter
1 square baking chocolate	=	1 ounce chocolate
2 ¼ cups packed brown sugar	=	1 pound brown sugar
3 ½ cups confectioners sugar	=	1 pound confectioners sugar
1 cup grated cheese	=	4 ounces cheese
4 cups diced cooked chicken	=	one 3 ½ -pound chicken
3 cups sliced carrots	=	1 pound carrots
½ cup sliced celery	=	1 rib celery
½ cup chopped onion	=	1 medium onion
1 cup chopped green pepper	=	1 large green pepper
2 teaspoons grated lemon peel	=	1 medium lemon
3 tablespoons lemon juice	=	1 medium lemon
2 tablespoons grated orange peel	=	1 medium orange
⅓ cup orange juice	=	1 medium orange

GENERAL INSTRUCTIONS

TRANSFERRING PATTERNS

When entire pattern is shown, place a piece of tracing paper over pattern and trace pattern, marking all placement symbols and markings. Cut out traced pattern.

When one-half of pattern is shown, fold tracing paper in half and place fold along dashed line of pattern. Trace pattern, marking all placement symbols and markings. Cut out traced pattern; open pattern and lay it flat.

SEWING SHAPES

1. Center pattern on wrong side of one fabric piece and use a fabric marking pencil or pen to draw around pattern. DO NOT CUT OUT SHAPE.
2. Place fabric pieces right sides together. Leaving an opening for turning, carefully sew pieces together directly on pencil line.
3. Leaving a ¼″ seam allowance, cut out shape. Clip seam allowance at curves and corners. Turn shape right side out. Use the rounded end of a small crochet hook to completely turn small areas.
4. If pattern has facial features or detail lines, use fabric marking pencil or pen to lightly mark placement of features or lines.

HOW TO STENCIL

1. Trace pattern onto tracing paper. Use transfer paper to transfer design to center of tagboard. Use craft knife to cut out stencil.
2. (Note: Use removable tape to mask any cutout areas on stencil next to area being painted.) Hold or tape stencil in place while stenciling. Use a clean, dry stencil brush for each color of paint. Dip brush in paint and remove excess paint on a paper towel. Brush should be almost dry to produce a good design. Beginning at edge of cutout area, apply paint in a stamping motion. If desired, shade design by stamping additional paint around edge of cutout area. Carefully remove stencil and allow paint to dry.

MINI PILLOW

1. Fold a length of jute in half. Referring to Fig. 1, pin fold on back of one stitched piece at center top edge of stitched area.

Fig. 1

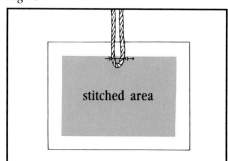

stitched area

2. (Note: Use 2 strands of floss and work Running Stitch over and under 1 fabric thread.) Place stitched pieces wrong sides together. Leaving an opening for stuffing and being careful

to catch jute in stitching, work Running Stitch 2 fabric threads from edges of design. Lightly stuff pillow with fiberfill. Use Running Stitch to sew final closure.
3. Trim pillow 6 fabric threads from Running Stitch, being careful not to cut jute. Remove fabric threads to within ⅛″ of stitched line.

FABRIC BAG

1. To determine width of fabric needed, add ½″ to finished width of bag; to determine length of fabric needed, double the finished height of bag and add 1½″. Cut fabric the determined width and length.
2. With right sides together and matching short edges, fold fabric in half; finger press folded edge (bottom of bag). Using a ¼″ seam allowance and thread to match fabric, sew sides of bag together.
3. Press top edge of bag ¼″ to wrong side; press ½″ to wrong side again and stitch in place. Turn bag right side out unless following Step 4.
4. For flat-bottom bag, match each side seam to fold line at bottom of bag; sew across each corner 1″ from end (Fig. 1). Turn bag right side out.

Fig. 1

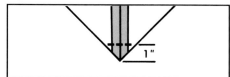

1″

GIFT BOX 1

Note: Use this technique to cover square or rectangular cardboard boxes that are already assembled such as shoe boxes, jewelry boxes, and some candy boxes.

1. For box top, refer to Fig. 1 to measure length and width of top (including sides). Add 1 ½ ″ to each measurement; cut wrapping paper the determined size.

Fig. 1

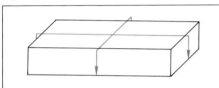

2. Place wrapping paper right side down on a flat surface; center box top, top side down, on paper. For one short side of box top, cut paper diagonally from corners to within ¹⁄₁₆″ of box (Fig. 2). Fold short edge of paper up and over side of top (Fig. 3); crease paper along folds and tape edge in place inside box. Repeat for other short side.

Fig. 2

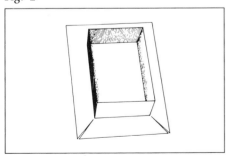

Fig. 3

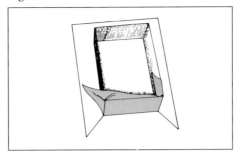

3. For one long side of box top, fold edges of paper as shown in Fig. 4; crease paper along folds. Fold paper up and over side of top; crease paper along folds and tape edge in place inside box. Repeat for other long side.

Fig. 4

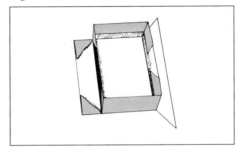

4. Repeat Steps 1 - 3 for bottom of box.

GIFT BOX 2

Note: Use this technique to cover cardboard boxes that are unassembled or are easily unfolded such as cake boxes or Chinese food take-out cartons.

1. Place wrapping paper right side down on a flat surface. Unfold box to be covered.
2. For a small box, apply spray adhesive to outside of entire box. Place box, adhesive side down, on paper; press firmly to secure.
3. For a large box, apply spray adhesive to bottom of box. Center box, adhesive side down, on paper; press firmly to secure. Applying spray adhesive to one section at a time, repeat to secure remaining sections of box to paper.
4. Use a craft knife to cut paper even with edges of box. If box has slits, use craft knife to cut through slits from inside of box.
5. Reassemble box.

CROSS STITCH

COUNTED CROSS STITCH

Work one Cross Stitch to correspond to each colored square on the chart. For horizontal rows, work stitches in two journeys (Fig. 1). For vertical rows, complete each stitch as shown in Fig. 2. When the chart shows a Backstitch crossing a colored square (Fig. 3), a Cross Stitch (Fig. 1 or 2) should be worked first; then the Backstitch (Fig. 5, page 124) should be worked on top of the Cross Stitch.

Fig. 1   Fig. 2

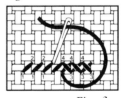

Fig. 3

Continued on page 124

GENERAL INSTRUCTIONS (continued)

QUARTER STITCH (¼ X)

Quarter Stitches are denoted by triangular shapes of color on the chart and on the color key. Come up at 1 (Fig. 4); then split fabric thread to go down at 2.

Fig. 4

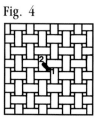

BACKSTITCH

For outline detail, Backstitch (shown on chart and on color key by black or colored straight lines) should be worked after the design has been completed (Fig. 5).

Fig. 5

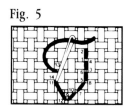

EMBROIDERY

FRENCH KNOT

Bring needle up at 1. Wrap thread once around needle and insert needle at 2, holding end of thread with non-stitching fingers (Fig. 1). Tighten knot; then pull needle through fabric, holding thread until it must be released. For a larger knot, use more strands; wrap only once.

Fig. 1

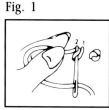

STRAIGHT STITCH

Come up at 1 and go down at 2 (Fig. 2).

Fig. 2

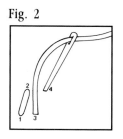

RUNNING STITCH

Make a series of straight stitches with stitch length equal to the space between stitches (Fig. 3).

Fig. 3

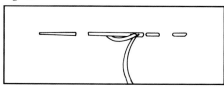

STEM STITCH

Following Fig. 4, come up at 1. Keeping the thread below the stitching line, go down at 2 and come up at 3. Go down at 4 and come up at 5.

Fig. 4

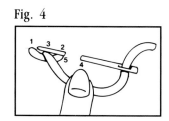

CREDITS

To Magna IV Engravers of Little Rock, Arkansas, we say thank you for the superb color reproduction and excellent pre-press preparation.

We want to especially thank photographer Mark Mathews of Peerless Photography, Little Rock, Arkansas, for his time, patience, and excellent work.

To the talented people who helped in the creation of some of the projects and recipes in this book, we extend a special word of thanks.

Sew Glad We're Friends, page 53: Kathy Middleton Elrod
Good Food, Good Friends, page 69: Polly Carbonari
Jointed Cat, page 107: Sandy Belt

Pork 'N' Bean Bread, page 109: Caroline Flaczynski
Barbecued Peanuts, page 117: Donna Lownds

We extend a sincere thank you to the people who assisted in making and testing the projects in this book: Pat Johnson, Catherine Hubmann, Karen Tyler, Barbara Hodges, Susan McDonald, and Laurie Terpstra.

RECIPE INDEX